WHAT YOUR DOG KNOWS

WHAT YOUR DOG KNOWS

Tap into your dog's intelligence through
the world of canine cognition

SOPHIE COLLINS

METRO BOOKS
NEW YORK

METRO BOOKS
New York

An Imprint of Sterling Publishing Co., Inc.
1166 Avenue of the Americas
New York, NY 10036

ISBN 978-1-4351-6566-3

For information about custom editions, special sales,
and premium and corporate purchases,
please contact Sterling Special Sales at 800-805-5489
or specialsales@sterlingpublishing.com.

Manufactured in China

2 4 6 8 10 9 7 5 3 1

www.sterlingpublishing.com

Design and illustrations by Alyssa Peacock

"Dogs do speak, but only to those who know how to listen."
—**Orhan Pamuk,** *My Name Is Red*

CONTENTS

INTRODUCTION

If you're a dog owner, you probably live as closely with your dog as with any other member of your family. You share much of your daily life, you play together, you spend downtime relaxing together, and almost half of dog owners are even happy to have their dog sleep on their bed. But how much do you know about what really goes on inside your dog's head? Have you ever spent much time thinking about what he sees, smells, and hears? Do you assume that his senses are more or less the same as yours?

A WORTHWHILE SUBJECT

The scientific study of the domestic dog used to be extremely rare, perhaps because dogs weren't considered "wild" or "natural" enough to be rewarding subjects for scientific research. Today, that's all changed; over the last two decades research into dogs' consciousness and intelligence, from being rather neglected, has become astoundingly popular. Universities are opening canine cognition labs all over the world, and exploring different aspects of dogs' behavior and cognition is the most fashionable research ticket around. It seems that, after many millennia living together, we've finally become curious about how dogs think and what their lives are like. And our view is consequently broadening beyond the frankly anthropomorphic, "My dog experiences things and feels things in much the same way as I do." Today, the view we have of dogs is a closer reflection of the truth: the best friend who shares so many aspects of your life has a consciousness so radically different from yours that it's hard to even imagine yourself into his furry head.

What Your Dog Knows takes an accessible overview of what some of this new research has taught us about dogs. It questions and debunks the dated notion that the dog was really "the wolf in the house"; dogs and wolves may share identical DNA, but we now have proof that domestication has wrought plenty of changes in the essential nature of dogs. They are very far from simply being wolves with softer fur.

WHAT IS IT LIKE TO BE A DOG?

The first section of the book examines the canine senses chapter by chapter, looking at the astounding superiority of your pet's sense of smell (could you detect a teaspoonful of sugar in a body of water equivalent to a couple of Olympic-sized swimming pools? Your dog could!), as well as his hearing (not only is it super sharp, but it's aided by amazing swiveling ears that catch even the faintest traces of sound), and at the various ways in which dogs' sight varies from ours. It questions whether your dog could possibly be psychic—a popular if minority view that seeks to explain some of the more extraordinary canine abilities—and looks at what a view of the world informed by smell rather than sight might be like.

WHAT DO WE REALLY KNOW ABOUT DOGS?

Having taken a tour around your dog's senses, the second section of the book looks at the current canine cognition picture—where the research is, what we know, and what we don't yet know. It tells the story of studies into canine cognition from the very beginning, going all the way back to Charles Darwin and taking you forward to the most recent manifestations: dogs who are happy to sit motionless in an MRI scanner for scientists to see just what their brains can tell us, and others who can apparently identify their owners from pictures, and still others who, in tests, were found to prefer "trustworthy" people to sneaky ones.

We then move into practical territory, offering a guide to your dog's body language and looking at just how nuanced the ways in which he expresses himself can be, from the tilt of his ears to the wag of his tail. Learn to see when he's stressed and apprehensive (or downright fearful), when he's ready for a game, and when he's tired or grouchy. There's even a section that looks at his different bark patterns and what they mean.

The final chapters offer a whole range of games and activities to try with your dog, including exercises to test how tuned in your dog is. You can have your own cognition lab at home, testing him for his empathy (does he yawn when you do?), his smarts (can he count, and does he recognize a range of different things by their names?), and his ability to read people.

Finally, we round things off with activities to deepen your bond with your dog, from a homemade agility course to an improvised nosework exercise and a ten-minute-a-day commitment to trying different things together. Now you know so much more about how he works, you can test out his abilities with a whole new range of experiences.

SECTION ONE
LOOKING AT A DOG'S WORLD

If you met someone from another universe and they asked you what your world was like, what would you say? How would you describe Earth? You'd probably start by talking about how it looks visually, what you can see around you in shapes and colors. But if the alien turned to your dog and asked the same question (let's say they have the ability to communicate without speech), we know his reply would be very different. Almost certainly he'd begin by describing the smells of his world in a degree of detail that would amaze you, and he might go on to cover the difficulties of living cheek by jowl with another species that never altogether understands you!

This section looks at your dog's senses, and the view they give him of the world around him. It will give you some surprising insights into just what it might be like to experience life as a dog.

CHAPTER 1: A DOG'S-EYE VIEW

How can you get a glimpse of the world the way your dog sees it? We tend to estimate our dogs' skills in terms of how closely they approximate our own (nicknamed by some behaviorists as "Understands-Every-Word-I-Say" syndrome), but to appreciate how special dogs really are, we need to realize how exceptional they are as a species in their own right.

THE WOLF IN THE HOUSE

Most people are relaxed about having a dog at home, but would you feel the same way about a wolf? It's unlikely. Yet dogs and wolves have identical DNA and they can crossbreed to create wolf-dogs. So are they as different as you might think? Is there a natural wolf in every dog?

The short answer is no, although, as you'd expect, researchers have consistently found it easier to find wolflike characteristics in breeds that bear a visual resemblance to wolves, such as German shepherds, and harder in breeds that don't, such as, well, pugs. Domestication began at a rather vague point in distant history, somewhere between fifteen and thirty thousand years ago, when two species, wolves and humans, began to see the mutual benefits they could bring one another, and the long-term result was the domesticated dog. Canine domestication, which happened first in the Middle East, was assumed to have been a long process, over centuries, or even millennia, rather than decades, although experiments since have suggested that it may have been quicker than originally believed.

How did it work? It's most likely that at the beginning the animals self-selected: wolves that were naturally more open to human contact, and thus less inclined to avoid it, began to accept food from and then perhaps work with humans to defend their cattle and sheep (rather than seeing herding animals as prey), ultimately taking a place by the hearth. They saw advantages in being cooperative, rather than purely self-reliant, and, as these tamer wolf-dogs tended to mix among themselves, like gradually bred with like to strengthen the characteristics that today we think of as "dog" rather than "wolf."

DMITRY BELYAEV AND THE FOX EXPERIMENT

Belyaev was a scientist and a geneticist in the Soviet Union. He was curious about key aspects of domestication, in all species, and decided to explore whether a speed-breeding program could produce the characteristics of tame animals, conducting one of the longest-running animal experiments ever. He chose silver foxes (shown here below) as his available subjects. Starting in 1959, a sample of over 100 animals was offered food and gentle handling daily. Those that seemed more open to it, and appeared more readily habituated to humans, were chosen to breed from.

The results were remarkably swift. Within ten breeding generations a fifth of the foxes' young were exhibiting "tame" features, and within twenty the proportion had gone up to over a third. By 1964 the tamer foxes were seen to wag their tales when familiar humans approached, and by the mid-1970s, the tamest would come when called. A part-domesticated state had been achieved in under 20 years.

WHY DOES DOMESTICATION MATTER?

Why does the fact that today's dogs are tamed from a true wild state matter in our understanding of them? Since the days of Darwin, scientists have understood that domesticated animals have different qualities to wild ones. Some of these qualities are visible: tamed animals tend to have soft floppy ears; their tails are shorter and often curl; and their coats may be softer. Others are behavioral: tamed animals are generally less fearful of the unfamiliar and more prepared to explore new territory, and they produce less adrenaline, the fight-or-flight hormone. These behaviors help them to live alongside people, without really blunting their natural sensory gifts.

Domestication is believed to have had other, less desirable effects. A study at the University of California in 2015 concluded that the narrowing of the wolf gene pool during the process of domestication meant that dogs inherited more damaged or harmful gene variants than were found in wild populations, and that these variants increased when dogs, already domesticated, were bred down further for specific traits. The study reinforced the widely held view that mixed-breed dogs, which draw from a wider gene pool, are healthier, while those bred for narrow and very particular characteristics may inherit a less welcome set of tendencies that can compromise long-term health.

THE DOG—WOLF EXPERIMENT

That dogs and wolves respond very differently to people was neatly shown by an experiment carried out between 2001 and 2003 at Eötvös Loránd University in Hungary. A large group of wolf cubs and puppies, raised from birth in exactly the same circumstances, were given a number of tasks to carry out, with food offered as a reward. In some, it wasn't actually possible for the animal to get to the food unaided. The wolves didn't recognize this; they would carry on, fruitlessly trying to reach the prize independently. The dogs, though, after trying for a minute or two, would start to look to "their" human for help, making eye contact. They recognized that humans could be used in problem solving, whereas the wolves, despite having been raised in exactly the same environment, didn't see it.

UNDER THE SKIN

Dogs are very able and very adaptable. As a result, humans focused for a long time on what dogs could be taught to do with their natural abilities, rather than watching what they chose to do for themselves. There was less interest in trying to find out what it's actually like to *be* a dog. Today, though, canine cognition is rapidly on the rise as a subject for research and experiment. And the more widely it is studied, the more conventional ideas of how we can measure both intelligence and cognitive processes will be questioned.

One barrier to gaining insight into what it might be like to be a dog is the way in which humans define intelligence. This question was addressed by the famous biologist Frans de Waal in his theory of the "biological ladder," a hierarchy of classification that places humans at the top (i.e., the most intelligent) and other creatures below them. In this hierarchy, intelligence is gauged as the ability to devise and execute solutions to problems, and then to analyze the results. Increasingly, though, cognition studies across a whole range of species have presented a much more complicated picture— less of a ladder and more of a dense, knotty network of abilities, which are defined by needs, expectations, and motivation.

HUMAN VS. CANINE REALITIES

Our reality is bound to be quite different from what is real to a dog. A dog has a different sensory system (more of that in the following chapters), so even experiences shared with a human can't seem the same to him. And while we're learning more about dogs, there are still large gray areas where we don't know much at all: How do dogs' memories work? Are they able to anticipate the future? Does a dog's dependence on humans mean that he's "smarter," as we might understand the term, than a wolf, or has a loss of independence actually made him dumber? And how would you measure it all, anyway? It is only natural that humans would make links to another species in terms of shared capabilities, but scientists now believe we'll learn more by looking at the differences.

DID YOU KNOW. . .

Dogs have learned the best ways to get what they want and need—to feel safe, to be fed, and to have shelter. The trade-off is that they're dependent on people. One increasingly popular line of thinking with cognition experts is that it's a two-way arrangement: dogs are using people just as much as the other way around.

HOW MUCH DO YOU KNOW ABOUT YOUR DOG?

Most owners already know quite a lot about dogs and about their dog, or dogs, in particular. How's your general knowledge about dogs, though? Here's the current thinking on some of the most commonly asked questions, including some useful (and some not so well-known) facts.

Q: HOW COMPLICATED IS A DOG'S PHYSIOLOGY?

A: Dogs have all the same physiological systems as other mammals, although their physiology is more complex in some ways. For example, a dog's skeleton has over 100 more bones than a human's (averaging out at 319 to your 206, and varying a little depending on the specific breed). Temperature-wise, your dog is hotter than you: our standard body temperature is around 99°F (37°C), while your dog's will be somewhere between 101°F and 102.6°F (38.3–39.2°C). Your dog's digestion is much slower than yours, and his stomach is far more acid. This is one reason why your dog is able to eat things that you would not, including rotten food and things you consider inedible, without necessarily suffering serious digestive consequences. His acid stomach is designed to cope with more hostile bacteria than yours.

Q: WHY DO DOGS LOOK SO DIFFERENT FROM EACH OTHER? HOW CAN A CHIHUAHUA AND A BULLMASTIFF BELONG TO THE SAME SPECIES?

A: More than any other animal, dogs have been bred selectively to do particular jobs, some over a very long period. *Canis lupus familiaris* proved uniquely adaptable, growing to match the requirement for a vast range of functions, from hunting prey (from elks to rats), to pulling loads and even to serving as toys, in the guise of lapdogs. While we may find it hard to see the "dog" inherent in some widely disparate breeds, and great differences in size, dogs apparently recognize other dogs as belonging to the same species, even when one is a wolfhound and another a chihuahua. Large dogs may even handicap themselves to make it possible to play with much smaller ones.

Q: ALL DOG OWNERS KNOW THAT DOGS CAN THINK, BUT CAN THEY USE REASON?

A: We know that they can reason and deduce to a limited extent, the most frequent comparison being that they have the deductive development of a human two-year-old. Studies have confirmed that they can use inferential reasoning—that is, if they know two different things, they can fill in the third. Here's an example: a dog is shown a toy, which is then hidden under one of two identical boxes. The boxes are rapidly switched around, so the dog no longer knows which box the toy might be under. When the researcher lifts one of the boxes and the toy isn't under it, the dog will go directly to the other and tip it over to get the toy. So the dog knows where the toy isn't, and his reasoning leads him to the knowledge of where the toy is. An area of growing interest currently is the degree to which dogs can reason independently of humans. It's much harder to research accurately, as, by definition, humans are involved in deciding what to test! We definitely don't know the whole story, though, and dogs retain the capacity to surprise us with their abilities.

. . . .

Q: DO SMART DOGS MAKE GOOD PETS?

A: This is an interesting one. All behaviorists have plenty of anecdotes about owners who are thrilled that they have a super-smart dog. Actually, smart dogs can be the hardest pets to own—they're the ones that usually need to be kept occupied, lest they direct their intelligence to something you *don't* want them to do. An example of behaviorists' humor is their "too bad" response to the owner who tells them their pet is a canine genius. From most owners' points of view, it is probably more important that a dog is connected and reliable.

Q: ARE SMART DOGS GOOD AT EVERYTHING?

A: A 2016 experiment carried out at the London School of Economics looked at whether dogs who had been found to be smart in one way (say, finding their way around a barrier to locate a food treat) would prove to be equally bright in other kinds of tests, such as following the direction of someone pointing, and working out where something is by being shown where it isn't, and so on. The "testees" were sixty-eight border collies, a breed broadly acknowledged to be both exceptionally clever and receptive to training. The findings showed that the smartest dogs, the ones who were fast and accurate on the first test, then tended to go on to stand out at all the others, across a range of abilities. It seems that smart dogs tend to be good all-rounders.

CHAPTER 2: A DOG'S SENSES—SIGHT

It's natural that dogs' astounding sense of smell tends to take top billing when we think about their senses, but their sight comes a worthy second. Although their eyes seem quite similar to ours in structure—like ours, the canine eye has a cornea, lens, and retina—they also have some key differences. Like other species that developed the skills to make them successful hunters, dogs are far more attuned to movement and contrast than to color and detail.

HOW DOGS SEE

The fact that dogs see colors less distinctly than humans do, but movements better, is down to a different balance of the types of cells in their eyes—the rods and cones. Both these cell types are situated in the eye's retina, and both are light-sensitive, but they have different functions.

Rods aren't useful for seeing color, but they are sensitive to changes in the level of light and are good for making out shapes and movement. They're particularly helpful when the eye is trying to see in dim light. Cones are used for color perception and in making out fine detail. Human eyes have around six million cone cells, comprising three types, with each type responsive to a different wavelength of light. As a result, they can see a full spectrum of color, which is known as trichromatic vision. Dogs, on the other hand, have just two types of cone cells, and far fewer of them—around 1.2 million—so, while your dog can see color, he will have difficulty in distinguishing between some shades. The effect is similar to the vision of a human with red/green color blindness.

The balance goes the other way when it comes to rods. While we don't have an exact count of how many rods there are in the typical dog's eye, we know that it's substantially more than the human total of around 120 million. This means that a dog's sensitivity to light, as opposed to color, is around five times better than a human's.

Dogs also have something that humans don't: a reflective layer behind the retina called the *tapetum lucidum*, which raises the level of light that the light-sensitive cells can use. It's the *tapetum lucidum* that you can see when your pet's eyes glow a reflected green in the dark.

DID YOU KNOW. . .
Although red remains a perennially popular choice for dog toys, next time you're treating your pet, try picking something in blue or yellow instead. He'll find it much easier to see against green when you're playing outside.

EYES IN THE BACK OF HIS HEAD

While humans have a tiny depression at the back of the retina called the fovea, which is used to process light directly to the cone cells, dogs have a strip densely packed with receptors that goes right across the retina, known as the visual streak. The fovea helps us to see fine detail, while the visual streak gives the dog much stronger peripheral vision and helps him to see things better out of the corner of his eye. His field of vision is a broad 270°, against the 180–190° of most humans. You'll notice this if you watch a dog following something he's interested in—maybe another animal running— across a wide panorama in front of him. He can follow it with his eyes for a very broad sweep before he has to move his head.

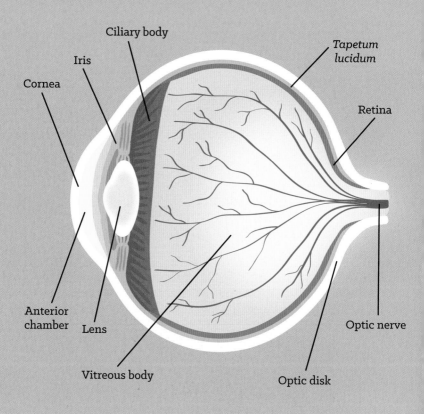

Ciliary body

Iris

Cornea

Tapetum lucidum

Retina

Anterior chamber

Lens

Vitreous body

Optic disk

Optic nerve

PREDATOR OR PREY?

Predator species, such as dogs or humans, have eyes placed on the front of their heads, while prey animals, such as sheep, have eyes set to the side. Front-facing eyes allow for binocular vision, meaning that a hunter can judge depth and distance accurately, thus giving him the best chance of chasing down his prey, while eyes on the side of the head offer all round peripheral vision, allowing a grazing animal to spot a predator, even if it is coming from behind. Although dogs have excellent peripheral vision for predators, it does not match that of typical prey.

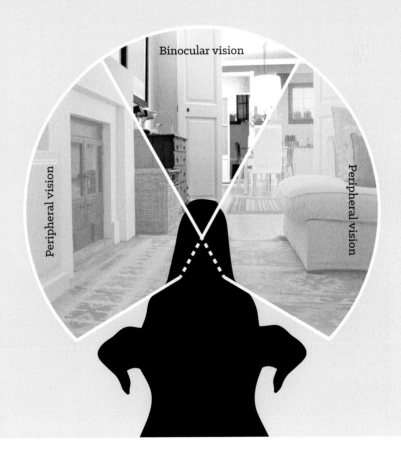

Binocular vision

Peripheral vision

Peripheral vision

Your dog's vision is affected by what breed he is. Not all the capabilities described on the previous page apply to flatter-faced, short-nosed (brachycephalic) dogs, such as bulldogs or pugs. Their flatter skull structure means that their eyes face directly forward, and they don't have the peripheral vision of longer-nosed breeds, such as German shepherds or Labradors.

Dogs are naturally crepuscular—that is, they're more active at the beginning and end of the day than during the midday hours—and it's probable that their sight evolved in the way it did to help them to hunt effectively in low light. It was more important to a dog's survival that he be able to see movement in poor light than to make out fine distinctions in color clearly. If your dog has a high prey drive, you will notice this when you take him out at dusk: he will spot the tiniest rustling movement in the undergrowth even as you struggle to make anything out in the failing light. And you'll notice, too, that color is imperceptible in very dim light, so finely tuned color vision becomes useless.

SEEING IN COLOR

Although we now know that dogs can see in color, until recently it was believed that they were color-blind. In any experiments with dogs, scientists were careful to use items where color wasn't relevant to the outcome. Research in the early 2000s proved that dogs could see color, but only within a limited spectrum, and it was assumed that they didn't really use their ability to distinguish colors in any meaningful ways.

That assumption changed as a result of a small experiment carried out in Russia in 2012. The researchers only used eight dogs, so the study was a very limited one. Its aim, though, was to prove that dogs could not only see color, but would also be able, when tested, to use color to gain a preferred outcome.

HOW THE EXPERIMENT WORKED

There were several stages, each taking place several times a day over a number of days. Two boxes, each containing a food treat, were put in front of the dogs, but only one was unlocked, so the dog could get at the treat inside. Each box had one of four different-colored paper disks in front of it, either dark yellow, light yellow, dark blue, or light blue.

In the first tests, the disks put in front of the boxes were a two-color dark/light combination—either light blue and dark yellow or dark blue and light yellow. Across ten days, the colors weren't varied, and the treat to which the dog could gain access was always in the box behind the same color. So a dog would learn, say, that the accessible box would always be behind the dark blue paper disk, not the light yellow one.

After ten days, when the dogs had gotten used to the test and were invariably going to the box under which they knew the treat was hidden, the researchers changed the colors. Now, the boxes were marked by disks of two new colors, and the dog that always went to the dark blue disk was given an option between dark yellow and light blue. If he made his choice according to the brightness of the disk, he'd go for the dark yellow; if, however, he was picking by color, he'd choose the light blue.

The results were fairly conclusive: over 70 percent of the time, a far higher percentage than would be dictated by chance, the dogs picked by color. If they'd become used to dark blue yielding up the treat, they'd choose the light blue disk on the later test, while if light yellow had resulted in success, they'd pick the dark yellow disk when retested.

Later, larger experiments confirmed the results: not only can dogs see color, but they can, when given an incentive, "think" color, too.

DOES YOUR DOG KNOW YOUR FACE?

How does your dog recognize you? Does he know how you look, or is he more focused on how you smell? And can he tell the mood you're in from your face alone? There's been comparatively little research in this area, but some recent work argues that your dog may not only recognize your face when he sees it on a screen but can also tell how you're feeling.

A study at the University of Helsinki in 2015 took thirty-one dogs of thirteen different breeds—twenty-three of which were domestic pets and eight of which were dogs kept in kennels—and sat them down in front of computer screens on which a whole range of faces, both canine and human, were shown in succession. The first thing it discovered is that, when it comes to faces, dogs show a clear preference for those of other dogs, and seemed more engaged in studying them for expression. That's not so surprising: one's own species is invariably going to be more familiar and thus easier to understand.

THE EYES HAVE IT

The "gaze" patterns—the parts of the faces looked at first, and the amount of time spent looking at individual features—that the dogs displayed, whether they were looking at human or dog faces, was quite similar to the patterns exhibited by people in the same sorts of tests. Generally, dogs, like people, look at the eyes first and spend the most time looking at them, then travel around the other features, looking most closely at the mouth. As for recognizing mood, when angry faces were shown, dogs looked carefully at other dogs with threatening expressions, but tended to look away, in apparent avoidance, from humans who looked angry.

The pets scored higher than the kennel dogs when it came to spending time on human faces and expressions, and could even recognize faces as faces when they were shown upside down, although it took them longer. Pet dogs showed the most interest when they saw their owners' faces on screen, spending longer looking at them, although it's impossible to say whether they actually "recognized" them, or whether they just seemed a bit more familiar than the other faces shown. Unsurprisingly, kennel dogs weren't as engaged with the human faces, instead spending more time on the faces of other dogs.

Dogs aren't just sensitive to eyes on screen; they concentrate on the eyes when meeting people, and anything that appears to magnify or obscure human eyes can be a source of apprehension and even fear. Glasses or, worse, reflective sunglasses, are a common source of phobias in dogs, probably because they seem to mimic and exaggerate the large, fixed pupils of the "hard eye" expression that dogs perceive as a threat. If a dog you're meeting for the first time seems intimidated for no obvious reason, make sure everyone removes their glasses; he may be apprehensive because he thinks he's being stared at.

DID YOU KNOW. . .

If dogs can recognize faces on screen, one may wonder what else they can see. Owners often report that their dogs watch television, with natural history programs the preferred genre. Can we know what dogs are really seeing when they watch TV, or is it all speculation? Well, there are some clues in the way the eye tracks movement. It seems likely that it's the movement rather than the subjects in the picture that appeals to dogs: they can auto-track natural movement on the screen in the same way that they can in real life. This means that if a rabbit or a deer is shown running on TV, the dog will have an instinctive recognition of the characteristic shapes and speeds of the movement and it's this that appeals to them, because it mimics real-life situations in a stimulating way.

SIGHT OR SMELL: WHAT DOGS FEAR

Do dogs smell the things that make them afraid or do they see them? Or is it a mixture of both senses that sends a fear message? Most people have been in a situation whereby a familiar dog has failed to recognize them, usually because they're huddled in thick winter clothing, they're wearing a hat, or perhaps, a surprisingly common fear, they're wearing sunglasses, and the "stranger" has provoked a volley of nervous barking. But surely, since dogs have such superior nose skills, that dog should have been able to smell that it was you?

How things look is certainly important to dogs, and many hate the unfamiliar. One well-known US behaviorist joked that the millennial fashion for hipster beards had doubled her workload of fearful dogs. But thinking that your dog should have recognized you, even though you were wearing something unfamiliar, is to impose human thinking patterns on the dog. In an age in which a lot of research and writing has ensured we are impressed by canine skills, it's easy to forget that their contexts are completely different from ours. Mixed signals ("she smells right, but she looks wrong") seem as likely in a dog's world to provoke a fearful response. And a lot of studies have established that while dogs understand the body shapes of other species, from cats to humans, they don't have any understanding of items that can be taken off, whether they are coats, hats, or sunglasses. Anything that covers the head, or obscures our facial expressions, seems to be especially intimidating. In an adult dog, these visual concerns can often be fixed by desensitizing, such as having men in hats or women in sunglasses feeding treats while taking hats and sunglasses on and off. And they can be forestalled altogether in most puppies by careful and thorough socialization during the key developmental stage, between eight and sixteen weeks.

DID YOU KNOW. . .
Puppies are less likely to become fearful adults if they're exposed to as wide a range of experiences as possible when they're between two and four months old. These should include meeting lots of different people, dogs, and other animals, in a number of different surroundings. Careful owners introduce unfamiliar things gradually and do their best to ensure that new experiences are managed.

SCARY VET

Of course, not all dogs hate vet visits. If they've been carefully habituated to them from puppyhood, many enjoy a trip to the vet. But for the dogs that do fear them, it may not be the sight of unfamiliar white coats or the sensation of being handled by strangers that triggers the fear; it's just as likely to be the smell of the veterinary office. One of the commonest jobs in a vet's daily workload will be to clear the blocked anal glands of at least one (more likely several) dogs, and the liquid inside them is the same liquid that dogs instinctively evacuate when very frightened. If your dog was apprehensive on entering the veterinary office, this is one of the smells that won't help calm his nerves.

SIGHTHOUNDS: NATURE'S CANINE EXCEPTIONS

If you have a sighthound, you'll already know that there's a group that proves the exception to the led-by-the-nose rule of most dogs. Sighthounds have the same refined sense of smell as other dogs, but the group encompasses all the breeds that have been developed, sometimes through centuries of breeding, purely to hunt by sight.

The group includes whippets, greyhounds, salukis and borzois, Afghan hounds, and Pharaoh hounds, which are some of the most ancient dog breeds around. Even the unaccustomed eye can see that these dogs are bred to run. Historically, they were typically used to hunt in open country, from flat farmland to desert, where they could run down everything from hares to antelopes.

Long-legged and slender, streamlined and aerodynamic in shape, sighthounds have a turn of speed that's unrivaled. Some of the earliest art depicts sighthounds, and the silhouette of the lean racing dog is remarkably recognizable down the centuries: rock paintings over eight thousand years old in Tassili N'Ajjer, in Algeria, show a pack of greyhounds (or something

very like them) bringing down horned animals, while dogs equally similar to today's Pharaoh hounds are shown as hunting companions on the walls of ancient Egyptian tombs.

Sighthounds have the broadest visual streak of any breeds, and their alertness to the movement of any potential prey is incredibly high. They have long been highly valued as status symbols: in the 16th century, at a time when hunting with hounds was the mark of every young aristocrat, a good sighthound could command an extraordinarily high price. In Britain, one hound was recorded as changing hands for 240 pennies, the equivalent of $3,125 (£2,500) today.

DID YOU KNOW. . .

The speediest sighthounds can outrun most animals. The record for the fastest greyhound stands at over 50 miles per hour (81kph). That's as fast as a lion or a Thomson's gazelle going at full stretch. It still falls behind the speediest animal on earth, the cheetah, which runs at speeds of around 70 miles per hour (113kph).

CHAPTER 3: A DOG'S SENSES—SMELL

There is one thing that everyone knows: all dogs have an exceptional sense of smell. Stories of outstanding sniffing feats abound, but how do they do it, and why are some dogs even better at sniffing out specific scents than others? Is it a natural gift, or do dogs "learn" to smell? This chapter looks at what we know about this special sense.

A STANDOUT SENSE

It's far and away a dog's most powerful sense, so much so that it's hard for us to imagine how a dog smells. One often-heard anecdote has a dog identifying a single rotten apple in two million barrels of good apples through smell alone. Dogs' sense of smell is so much more accomplished than ours, and the statistics relating to it are so extraordinary that they're hard to absorb.

Not only is a person's sense of smell very weak compared to that of any dog, but it's also unpracticed: humans rely on their eyes rather than their noses to take stock of a situation. Yet, just as eyes must adjust to new circumstances and stimuli in order to provide the necessary information, noses must also adapt to constantly changing environments.

SCENT: THE FULL SPECTRUM

Not only do dogs have the power to smell across a huge range, but they can also distinguish between the things they smell. In general, humans don't have a problem separating items visually; when we see a stack of books, say, we know that it's both a stack and also a number of separate items. Asked to pick out a particular title from the pile, identified by the text on the spine or its color, we could do so without hesitating. However, unlike dogs, we can't do the same with a smell. One comparison that has been used by a number of dog specialists goes like this: if we pick up the scent of a savory soup, say, wafting out of a window, it's possible that we might be able to smell that it was a chicken soup, but we couldn't pick out the individual scents of chicken, carrots, leeks, and potatoes, and we certainly wouldn't be able to pull out and separately identify the thyme, salt, and pepper that underlie them. A dog could do that unhesitatingly. Tests have shown that he could separate them on his palate, too, just as, faced with a complicated fabric print, we might first appreciate the effect of the overall pattern, then enjoy picking out the details of different shapes and the subtleties of shades of color within the whole.

A DOG'S NOSE

How many times better is your dog's sense of smell than yours? Estimates range hugely—the number of sensitive cells can be counted, but exactly how powerful this makes the dog's experience can only be estimated. Some say it's ten thousand times better, others that it's one hundred thousand times. Whichever is closer to the truth, some practical examples taken from stories of professional sniffer dogs, whose living is earned by their nose power, are perhaps the easiest way to get an idea of how it feels:

• One dog smelled a block of marijuana that had been wrapped in several layers of heavy-duty plastic and suspended in a full tank of petrol.

• A pair of dogs on Puget Sound were trained to sniff out whale feces (finding it while still fresh is key to the study of whales living in the wild) and could track it from 1.2 miles (2km) away in deep ocean. The first tests failed because the researchers didn't follow the directions that the dogs gave, because they couldn't believe the extent of the dogs' sense of smell.

• In comparison tests, dogs used to sniff out the presence of cancer cells in humans have been proven equal to, or even more accurate, than scanners.

HOW IT WORKS: THE STRUCTURE OF A DOG'S NOSE

With all that proven ability, you'd expect dogs to have quite a complex nose structure, and you'd be right. Not only can they breathe in and out independently (and thus avoid mixing incoming smells up), they also have a special structure designed to focus on natural chemicals called pheromones—smells that we don't even consciously acknowledge—meaning that they are constantly using two separate, and largely unconnected, systems to process smells.

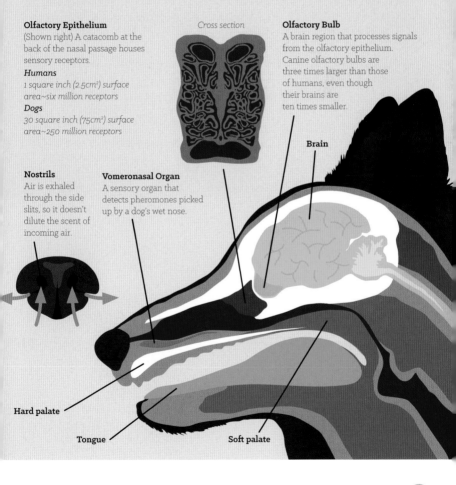

Olfactory Epithelium
(Shown right) A catacomb at the back of the nasal passage houses sensory receptors.
Humans
1 square inch (2.5cm²) surface area~six million receptors
Dogs
30 square inch (75cm²) surface area~250 million receptors

Cross section

Olfactory Bulb
A brain region that processes signals from the olfactory epithelium. Canine olfactory bulbs are three times larger than those of humans, even though their brains are ten times smaller.

Brain

Nostrils
Air is exhaled through the side slits, so it doesn't dilute the scent of incoming air.

Vomeronasal Organ
A sensory organ that detects pheromones picked up by a dog's wet nose.

Hard palate

Tongue

Soft palate

HOW DOGS SMELL

Look at a dog's nose and you'll see two nostrils, usually slightly damp. The moisture helps to "catch" passing scent molecules for the dog to inhale, and each nostril can wiggle independently, making the most of the smells around it. Like us, dogs use their noses for breathing as well as smelling; unlike us, they have the physical ability to keep the two functions separate. Just inside the dog's nostrils there is a fold of tissue that directs the air entering the nose. Air passes through the fine hairs lining the nostrils, the cilia, and a proportion of the air breathed in, around 12 percent, is directed into a recessed area, the olfactory epithelium, up at the back of the nose, where it is used for smelling. The rest of the air travels down to the lungs for the dog to breathe.

When the dog breathes out, airflow passes through the side slits of the nostrils, so that it doesn't contaminate or dilute the scent molecules in the air that the dog is breathing in through the larger central holes.

The olfactory epithelium is at the back of the nose, close to the brain. It's a dense maze of bony structures called turbinates, arranged in complicated surfaces and folds, and it houses an estimated average 250 million scent receptors (for comparison, humans have only 6 million). The turbinates have the capacity to sieve the scent molecules that enter the epithelium, grouping them according to their different chemical compositions. The receptors send electrical triggers to the dog's brain according to the chemical signals that the scent molecules set off, allowing the dog to analyze what he smells. A large area of the canine brain—some experts estimate as much as a third— is dedicated to "reading" what the nose collects.

A SECOND SYSTEM: THE VOMERONASAL ORGAN

The organ that the dog uses to scent pheromones, the vomeronasal organ (also called Jacobson's organ), is separate from the "ordinary" scenting system and is located just inside the nose, with an opening into the mouth. The receptors in the vomeronasal organ are adapted to the large molecules of pheromones. These don't usually have an obvious "scent" for the dog to take in; rather, they contain species-specific chemical "prompts," which are carried by the vomeronasal organ's own dedicated nerve system, traveling directly to the brain. The entire system operates entirely independently from the dog's other scenting system.

THE JOY OF SCENT

Knowing that our dogs have an incomprehensible, to us at least, sensitivity to scent molecules poses some puzzles. One often raised by dog owners is, if my pet has such a refined sensitivity to odors, why is it that he also seems to enjoy many truly horrible smells?

From vomit to feces, and rotting fish to rancid food remains, dogs fervently love all kinds of scents that revolt people, and they're prepared to submit them to an up-close examination that would make us retch. To a human, it's both funny and slightly disgusting to see their pet not only sniff something dead and rotten up close, but also visibly to "run" the scent across his palate, like an oenophile sniffing a rare vintage wine.

We can't tell exactly what it is that dogs like about noxious smells, and no experiment has offered a definitive answer, but one thing those smells have in common is that they're all extremely strong. Also, they are natural rather than artificial; it's noticeable that most dogs don't enjoy manmade "scented" products at all. Perfume and air freshener, for example, seem to make them sneeze, and most will turn their heads away if they encounter them up close.

ROLLING AROUND

In addition to sniffing at things we find revolting, many dogs, if they have the chance, will finish off the unexpected bonanza by rolling in whatever smelly and rotten treasure they have found. It's a routine that makes most dog owners sigh in resignation, but why do dogs do it? Is it the direct canine equivalent of anointing oneself in delicious perfume, or is there something else going on?

There's no definitive answer, but there are a number of theories among experts as to why dogs roll. Number one is the most obvious: to a dog, it smells good, and he'd like to have as much of the smell as he can get his paws on. Number two is the possibility that he's showing off: he wants to be around other dogs advertising that he has access to the best resources. Finally, dogs may cover their own natural scent with something stronger as a disguise, perhaps, historically, to help them when hunting prey. Most who've studied it agree that whatever prompts the rolling, it's probably a behavioral hangover from canines' wilder past.

The veteran dog expert Stanley Coren has offered one of the most appealing suggestions for why dogs roll. He suggested that strong and (to us) noxious scents have the same joyous appeal for a dog as a really loud Hawaiian shirt has for an exuberant vacationer.

FACEBOOK FOR DOGS

It's a question, often unspoken, that every dog owner has: why, with his super-refined sense of smell, does your dog always go straight for the rear end of every new dog he meets? What does the back end tell him that the front end wouldn't? And why is the pee and poop of other dogs of such paramount interest that, if encountered, it absolutely has to be sniffed?

We know that dogs aren't the same as us, and the classic butt sniff confirms it. They are so different, in fact, that a calm rear-end sniff is the politest way one dog can meet another, particularly on a first encounter. It's the handshake of the canine world. If your dog is a good mixer and socially confident, this is how he'll introduce himself. Face-to-face sniffing is actually the rude, overly direct approach, usually only practiced when dogs have already "met" nose to tail.

The reason for it is that the anal glands, plus any residual drops of pee, are the site of most of the information that a dog wants to know about another dog. The anal glands, two small, pea-sized sacs, are located just inside a dog's anus, and the liquid in them (which, incidentally, as anyone who has been to the vet to have their pet's anal glands expressed will testify, smells disgusting to humans) is your dog's unique scent-print, containing pheromones from both the apocrine and the sebaceous glands. A dog sniffing the area will pick up all sorts of pheromone information, which will be carried straight to the vomeronasal organ, and thence to the brain. The information ranges from the basic, such as the new dog's gender, to the more complex, including the dog's state of health, age, diet, and even the mood he's in.

Urine is the most common carrier of information when a dog isn't present. Not for nothing is it sometimes called pee-mail by dog owners. To a dog, it's a resource to be hoarded rather than used up all in one go; small "marking" pees will be left, particularly by male dogs, for other dogs to sniff all along the route of any walk, although quite why is less clear. Scientists who studied peeing habits as a means of territorial marking, as was originally believed, have drawn a blank, suggesting that constant marking is perhaps instead a residue of wolf behavior that isn't yet completely understood.

DID YOU KNOW. . .
When a dog smells another dog's feces, what he's sniffing is actually the anal gland secretions, a drop or two of liquid that the dog emits just after he poos. It is a small, powerful dose of chemicals dropped as an "I was here" indicator, and sometimes scuffed up with some vigorous scratching as an end gesture to the process.

BEST IN CLASS

Every dog is gifted when it comes to their sense of smell, but dog owners are often curious about where their pet ranks in the best-smeller charts. And academic researchers have long questioned whether dogs with outstanding scenting gifts always belong to the breeds that you'd expect. An ability to track is usually held to be the ultimate test of a dog's scenting skill.

Breed certainly has some bearing. For example, short-nosed, or brachycephalic, dogs invariably score less well in scent tests than other breeds. This makes sense: their flatter noses have less space for the complicated maze of turbinates that is so crucial to a dog's smelling ability. At the other end of the scale are the scenthounds, most of which, as the name implies, have been selectively bred not only for their ability to identify scents but also for their skill in selecting individual smells and tracking them. The group includes a range of sizes, from the dachshund and the beagle to the foxhound and the basset hound. Top of the tracking tree is the bloodhound, the undisputed Einstein of the canine scent world. Not only is the species believed to have 300 million scent receptors, well over the average number for a dog (around 250 million), but its physique also offers a number of other natural advantages. Bloodhounds have long flapping ears that wave scent molecules toward their noses, and deep wide muzzles with plenty of space for turbinates and broad passages to sweep air through. Not only that, but they're also very heavily muscled through the shoulders, allowing them to follow scent traces by holding their noses close to the ground for long periods without tiring, which is just as well, because a bloodhound can follow a trail for anything up to 130 miles (210km). They are also famous for being able to pick up old trails; bloodhounds have been recorded following trails that are over twelve days old.

THE ART OF TRACKING

Not much puts a keen tracking dog off the scent. An older scent will usually be "tracked"—technically, this means that it's followed from traces on the ground—while a fresh scent will more likely be "trailed," a more zigzagging process that follows the recent scent molecules that are still present in the air (when you see a dog put his nose up and sniff the air, he's more likely than not trying to pin down specific scent molecules). Contrary to popular belief, crossing water doesn't usually throw a skilled dog off the trail—he'll usually just pick the scent up on the other side.

TOP TEN TRACKERS

The dogs used worldwide for tracking a scent are surprisingly varied. These are the breeds that regularly make the top ten in tracking ability:

1. Bloodhound

2. Basset hound

3. Beagle

4. German shepherd

5. Labrador retriever

6. Belgian Malinois

7. Springer spaniel

8. Coonhounds *(this group includes six breeds: black-and-tan, bluetick, English, plott, redbone, and treeing walker)*

9. German shorthaired pointer

10. Pointer

THE SCENT DETECTIVES

One of the more controversial ways in which dogs have been used for their natural gifts has been in "scent lineups," in which a trained scenting dog is given an item left at a crime scene to sniff, then asked to pick out the culprit by smell from a lineup of containers, one of which contains a scent sample from the suspect, and the others samples from random individuals. However careful a criminal is about leaving trace evidence behind them, they can't eliminate their smell, the thinking goes, and the dog will be able to sniff them out. Over the last three decades, "evidence" gathered along these lines has been accepted in a number of countries, but even the greatest enthusiasts for dogs' scenting abilities admit that the method hasn't proved foolproof. While a research project in the Netherlands resulted in the dogs making their selections with 85 percent accuracy, things are less clear elsewhere. A debate over the unregulated ways in which some scent tests were held in Texas, combined with what many felt were disproportionate conviction rates arising from scent lineups alone, has led to a major legal row in the US.

Bloodhounds and German shepherds are the two breeds that have been used most often for scent lineups, and not even the doubters question their exceptional abilities. It seems, though, that humans aren't yet able to "read" exactly what the dogs are telling them with enough accuracy to make scent lineups a reliable way to sniff out the guilty.

DID YOU KNOW. . .

The American Kennel Club offers three levels of tracking tests for dogs. The starter level, called The Tracking Dog, requires the dog to follow a track 440–500 yards (400–450m) long, with a scent trail up to two hours old. By comparison, the third level, called Variable Surface Tracking, requires the dog to follow a track 600–800 yards (550–730m) long, with a number of turns in direction, and with a scent trail that can be up to five hours old. Only five percent of the dogs that enter level three emerge with a pass. A dog that passes all three levels gains the title of Champion Tracker.

THE WORLD'S SMALLEST POLICE DOG

When you think of a police dog, a German shepherd is probably the breed that springs to mind. But in Geauga County, Ohio, a chihuahua–rat terrier mix called Midge has been a member of the K-9 unit in the sheriff's department since 2006, when she joined the force at only three months old. Weighing in at eight pounds (3.6kg), she has proved the ideal size for squeezing into tiny spaces that her colleague, Brutus, a German shepherd, can't get near. Trained as a drug detection specialist—she can identify ten different types of drug— she's small enough to nose her way into almost any corner in which they could be hidden. Midge isn't unique, either; in 2010, Momo, also a chihuahua, debuted at search-and-rescue trials held in the western Japanese prefecture of Nara. Her test was to sniff a cap and then identify its owner in a lineup in under a minute, and she passed with flying colors.

PUTTING THEIR NOSES TO WORK

Distance tracking is one of the ways humans put dogs' noses to work. Dogs' flexibility and willingness to work together with humans in a team mean that today dogs are given all kinds of jobs, from sniffing out illegal substances to search and rescue, and even truffle hunting—the Lagotto Romagnolo (pictured below) is trained to sniff out truffles.

All these jobs call for specific scent training, sensitizing dogs to particular scents and teaching them to screen out distractions. Very broadly, though, the training follows the same pattern, whether a dog is being trained to sniff out explosives or drugs, or searching for survivors after a natural disaster. Scent training will be combined with other skills, such as cooperation and communication with a handler, and it will often start when puppies are just eight weeks old. The dogs may graduate from this initial training stage at around eighteen months. It's only at this point that they start to specialize and undergo more training in a particular field, such as search and rescue.

A DOG'S SCENTING LIFE

When you compare a dog's nose to a person's eyes, you come as close as you can to imagining how it might feel to smell as a dog. Our sense of sight offers us something of the range of abilities a dog's nose offers him. It's still hard to get your head around something so different from the human experience, though.

Imagine looking at a field the morning after snowfall. The snow is criss-crossed by the numerous tracks of the creatures that have walked across it overnight; birds, mice, voles, rabbits, weasels, and foxes may all have left their mark. You can see at a glance that lots of different animals have been there, but you can also track an individual animal by following the footprints over and under others, along a specific path. When a dog smells the same field, without the snow, we believe he'll have the same experience, but through the medium of scent molecules. He can't see the tracks with his eyes, but he'll immediately have a broad image of the number of animals that have tracked across the field recently, and if he focuses on an individual track, he'll be able to follow its scent in the same way you can follow it visually.

FOLLOWING A PATH

If we humans are out taking a walk, in woodland, for example, we tend to follow a path without diverging from it much. A bird-watcher might head off the beaten track, if they catch a glimpse of something they'd like a closer look at—the wing flash of a jay, say—and a plant enthusiast might take a detour, if they spot a rare woodland orchid. Dogs don't walk like us; off leash, they're heading off after things of interest all the time, sometimes things we can see (a rabbit rustling), often things we can't. If you have a particularly nose-led breed or individual, you'll have become used to him taking his own large and independent detours to track down particular points of scenting interests. If you think of his ability as both vocation and job, you'll probably come close to understanding what it means to him. It's something he's naturally gifted at, and it's also of absorbing mental interest.

WALKING THE WALK

The cognitive scientist Alexandra Horowitz, who has made a lifetime's study of dogs, including wonderful informed speculation on exactly what it might be like to be a dog, suggests taking a walk in your pet's footsteps and imagining his sensations, focusing on not only the smells, but also on what he sees (taking his height into consideration—even the tallest dog has a quite different viewpoint to a human one) and the layout of the landscape before him. It's always revealing to watch your dog closely. He'll offer plenty of clues as to what his walk is like for him. Watch for when he's distracted, when he's keen to get to a particular spot, when he's "reading" the signs of other dogs, and when he's leaving some signs of his own.

CHAPTER 4: A DOG'S SENSES—HEARING

Dogs have very acute hearing indeed, and it can also be selective: most owners are familiar with the pet that ignores a cement mixer in next-door's garden but goes on instant full alert at the sound of a packet of potato chips being opened downstairs. This chapter takes a closer look at how dogs hear sounds and across what range, and also at how they use their own noises to communicate.

HOW DOGS' EARS WORK

However a dog's ears look from the outside (and there's quite a range, from long, droopy, flapping ears to large pointy ones, and the button variety, with neatly folded tips), they all work in the same way inside. Design-wise, canine ears aren't much different from human ears, apart from one big factor: the muscular outer structure is extremely mobile, geared to proactively catch sound rather than simply receive it.

With eighteen muscles managing movement at the base of each ear (humans have just six), dogs are able to shift their ears around, rather than waiting passively for the sound to get to them. As you'll know if you've ever tried, directional ear wiggling isn't an option for a person. If humans want to hear something more clearly, they need to turn their heads so that their ears are facing directly toward the sound. For a dog, being able to swivel his ears freely offers a huge aural advantage. What's more, the flap of each canine ear can move independently, enabling the dog to take in sounds from two different directions at once.

Probably unsurprisingly, the dogs with the most acute hearing are those with the most wolf-like ears—in other words, those that are large, open, upright, and pointed. But the hearing of any dog, even one with long, floppy ears, is substantially better than that of any human. Studies estimate that dogs hear sounds up to four times farther away than humans can.

The mobility of dogs' ears means, too, that they will be alerted by noises we can't hear. Often, you'll see a dog's ears turn in the direction of a sound, such as an emergency siren, that you'll hear yourself only a few seconds later.

INSIDE THE EAR

Once a sound has been captured within a dog's ear, it passes down the opening of the ear canal, angling down to the eardrum, which is the start of the middle ear. Noise is received as vibrations, carried through the middle vestibular system (the three little bones known as the ossicles) to the cochlea, the curled tube in the inner ear, which turns the vibrations into nerve impulses, which are then posted along the auditory nerve for the brain to process.

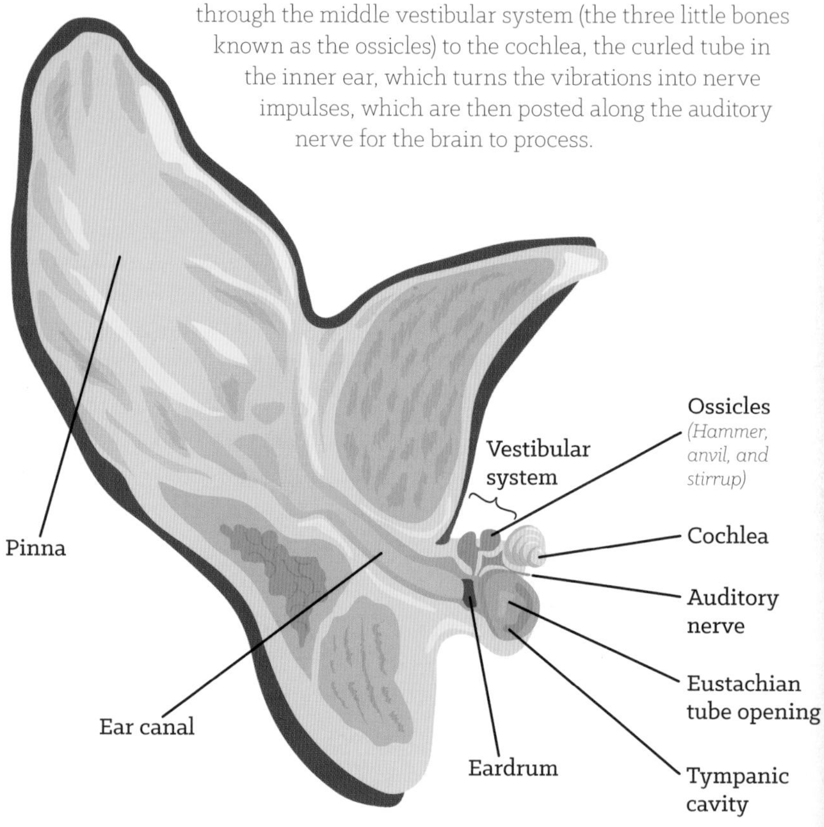

Pinna

Vestibular system

Ossicles
(Hammer, anvil, and stirrup)

Cochlea

Auditory nerve

Eustachian tube opening

Ear canal

Eardrum

Tympanic cavity

DID YOU KNOW. . .

Dogs are actually born with their ear canals closed. They are deaf until they are around three weeks' old, at which point the canals open and their hearing kicks in.

WHAT RANGE OF SOUND?

Dogs not only hear from farther away than humans, they also hear a different range of sounds. While their ability to hear lower-frequency sounds is close to that of humans, they can hear noises of a much higher pitch than people are able to. That's why a dog will respond to the sound of a whistle that the person blowing it can't hear at all.

THE STATISTICS OF HEARING

Noise is measured in vibrations per second, or hertz (Hz). Although a number of experiments have over the past sixty years been conducted with the aim of precisely measuring the range of sounds animals can hear, it has proved hard to get conclusive results. Obviously, an animal can't tell researchers exactly when a sound first becomes audible.

The experiments carried out specifically with dogs have involved the production of an increasingly loud noise to one side of a dog, with an automatic reward given as soon as he shows any awareness of that noise. Although the results are not universally recognized, nor are scientifically precise, they have been broadly adopted as a reasonably accurate guide. They judge that dogs' hearing falls in the range of between 67Hz (the lowest-pitched sounds) and 45,000Hz (the highest-pitched). By contrast, humans have a range of 64–23,000Hz.

By human standards, then, dogs have excellent hearing, but it's not necessarily exceptional, even in your living room, let alone in the animal kingdom as a whole—cats score higher, with a range of around 45–64,000Hz.

A HIGHER SALES PITCH

In 2011, some innovative advertisers spotted an unexploited opportunity offered by the hearing range of dogs: they produced the first TV commercial aimed at canine customers. Its cheerful soundtrack, consisting of music, conversation, and barking, was overlaid with another one, pitched too high for human ears to hear, which aimed to offer noises that would catch the attention of their dogs. In research, dogs had rushed to the screen, ears pricked, when it was played, and the director hoped that owners, charmed by the ad's effect on their pets, would rush just as fast to buy the pet food advertised. Despite getting plenty of press coverage, it isn't clear whether the innovation actually prompted a spike in sales.

For comparison, here are some estimated ranges for other animals or animal groups. As you might expect, the global record-breakers with the highest pitches have been judged as bats and cetaceans, with porpoises believed to have the ability to hear the highest-pitched sounds of all.

Porpoise: 75–150,000Hz

Horse: 55–33,500Hz

Rat: 200–76,000Hz

Rabbit: 360–42,000Hz

Mouse: 1000–91,000Hz

Bat: 2000–110,000Hz

Beluga whale: 1000–123,000Hz

CAN DOGS HEAR FEELINGS?

We may know quite a lot about the mechanics of a dog's hearing, but we know much less about what happens to the sound when it reaches his brain. It's an area of study that has intrigued scientists in recent years. One of the questions they have tried to answer is whether our pets understand our voices as both a practical and an emotional means of communication.

It's a subtle point. Since dogs live alongside us and have acted as companions to humans for thousands of years, we've come to assume that our pets understand our efforts at communication with them and feel a bond as a result of it. But simply knowing that a dog will react in a certain way when you cue him with specific sounds doesn't necessarily mean that he understands you "as a person."

BRAIN-PROCESSING EMOTION

Now, though, evidence has been found that dogs have a similar brain configuration to people when it comes to processing "social information," which means that your pet can recognize when you are happy or sad (something that dog owners would insist that they knew all along). In one experiment that proved the point, dogs were played different sounds, including those of people laughing and crying. Humans were tested alongside the dogs, and the same voice-sensitive areas of the brain in both humans and dogs were activated by the sounds.

The human–dog study, carried out at Eötvös Loránd University, Hungary, was particularly demanding because, in order to scan the brain, the dogs had to lie motionless in an MRI scanner, albeit only for a short time. It took twelve training sessions for each dog to lie still for long enough, but the rewards and attention levels were so good that by the end of the process the researchers reported that the dogs were clamoring to get into the scanner.

The results? When dogs hear us talking, they can separate the meaning of words with which they are familiar from the tone of voice in which they're spoken, and their brains analyze the two different components individually. As with humans, the left side of the brain processes the meaning of the words, while the right side processes the tone. Dogs have a proven response to emotion in the human voice, although, perhaps unsurprisingly, they responded even more strongly to the sounds made by other dogs.

WHY DOGS HEAR SO WELL

We're still finding out exactly what dogs hear, but there's general agreement that their fairly acute hearing is a result of the evolution from being predators: it benefited their predecessors to be able to both smell and to hear their prey at a distance. And with fast-moving prey, ranging from rats and rabbits to deer, very directional hearing was a strong asset in pinning down the location of food when out hunting.

THE NOISES YOU MAKE

Dogs are used to observing us very closely—far more so, in fact, than we usually notice. So if you want to teach a dog something new, you have to be very conscious of not sending mixed messages. And because the tone of what you say is at least as important to your dog as the words, the way you communicate with your dog is an important factor.

If you listen to the different noises dogs make themselves (more about that later on), you'll notice that higher, shriller sounds are exciting and act as a call to do something, whereas lower, deeper sounds slow things down. Your dog will hear the same qualities in your speech to him, so match your pitch to the message that you want to send.

For a requested action, short and clear is usually best, whereas if you want to stretch things out (for example, asking your pet to wait in a prolonged, "Stay"), long and low is likely to work better. Noises should be definite, not uncertain or vague. Dogs tend to send clear signals to one another and will appreciate the same from you.

ISSUING COMMANDS

- **Rising tone (up at the end, like a question), repeated**
  Works for: "Come!"—calling your dog; a request to action

- **Single, short, medium-pitched sound**
  Works for: "No," "Uh-uh"—a correction; a request to your dog to stop doing something

- **Single, short, loud sound**
  Works for: "Hey!"—a stop-doing-that-immediately correction (but don't overuse; this one is best for emergencies, so you don't want to wear it out)

- **Long, low, slow tone**
  Works for: "Staaaaay," "Waaaaait"—lower and slower call to inhibit action

GETTING IT WRONG

That's not your dog, it's you. There are a few simple mistakes that almost everyone makes when they're trying to teach their pet something new.

Noises

- Match the tone to the request

- Don't repeat yourself. Repeating a request means that your dog will eventually take their cue from the third or fourth repetition. This doesn't hold for times when you're asking a dog to act and go on acting—for example, see the "Come!" request, above. If your dog doesn't respond at the first time of asking, wait for a count of three before asking again.

- If you've used a short, sharp noise to stop your dog doing something, ideally you should move on immediately to redirect him to something that you do want him to do (preferably with an upbeat, rising-tone request).

Actions

- You've matched your tone to your request, so check that your body language matches the request, too—generally, leaning toward or looming over a dog will encourage him to back up, while leaning back or turning slightly away tends to encourage him to move forward.

NOISE-SENSITIVE DOGS

Why do some dogs calmly sleep through thunderstorms, while others
are reduced to a bag of nerves before the thunderclaps even start? Noise-
sensitive dogs can be made miserable by a whole range of sounds, but
thunderstorms and fireworks are at the top of the list. If your dog is one
of them, you'll probably have been recommended a whole raft of possible
"cures" (and with patience, most sound-fearful dogs can be desensitized
to at least some degree).

The reason some dogs are noise-sensitive isn't fully understood, but
sensitivity to noise can be a serious problem. A study of over five thousand
pet dogs undertaken in Norway in 2015 found that various factors might
affect whether or not a dog was sensitive to a range of noises, from fireworks
and thunderstorms to heavy traffic. Some breeds of the seventeen engaged
in the study seemed to be more likely to suffer than others (among the least
noise-sensitive were pointers, boxers, and Great Danes), and female dogs
were 30 percent more likely to be affected than males. Unsurprisingly, dogs
that were noise-sensitive were also more likely to suffer from separation
anxiety and to show greater timidity in situations that were new to them,
and older dogs, too, tended to find loud noises harder to cope with.

WAYS TO HELP

The good news is that there are several ways in which owners can help to desensitize their dogs. Those with proven success include:

- **Creating a safe place**
  Left to himself, a frightened dog may find his own space, be it under a bed or behind a sofa. Making a covered, dark den that he can establish as his safe space gives him somewhere to go when the noise starts.

- **Desensitization**
  The dog behaviorist Patricia McConnell has written widely about helping her own dogs with thunder phobia by creating an association between thunderstorms and something the dogs loved (treats or play, which she calls "thunder treats"). This isn't a speedy fix, but there is plenty of evidence that, applied consistently, it works.

- **Swaddling**
  Wrapping the dog's body tightly, either in a tight-fitting shirt produced specifically for dogs or in a more improvised tightly fitted T-shirt, reassures some dogs.

- **Pheromone and sound therapies**
  The first can be bought as a plug-in diffuser and imitates the pheromones found in mother dogs when suckling their puppies; the second consists of music that has been developed to reduce anxiety in dogs.

DOG-TO-DOG: WHEN DOGS TALK

What dogs hear is only one aspect of dog communication. What they say is just as important, and most dogs have a repertoire of barks, whines, growls, and other less immediately definable sounds that will gradually become familiar to their owners. Some are involuntary reactions, while others will be deliberate communication, and efforts to categorize which is which, and what individual barks really mean, could keep the dedicated dog "interpreter" very busy.

DIFFERENT TYPES OF BARKS

Despite its interest as a field for study, there has been comparatively little research into the vocalization of dogs. There have, though, been plenty of efforts to categorize dogs' different barks. The variables of barking are the pitch and length of the individual bark and how often it's repeated. If you want to try categorizing the different barks your own dog makes, one of the most straightforward methods comes from the highly regarded Norwegian trainer Turid Rugaas. She has divided dogs' barks into six broad categories: noises that express excitement, warning, fear, guarding, frustration, and, finally, "learned" barking. Listening carefully to the same dog every time he barks, and noting the circumstances he barks in, is the quickest way to get your ear in and to recognize his unique voice and tone.

A bark's sound will vary, of course, depending on the dog. The key identifier of a human voice is a mixture of the words used and the tone they're spoken in, and barks can be categorized in a similar way. For humans the message is conveyed through words, and its urgency is expressed in the tone. With dogs, the pitch is in part dependent on the breed of dog. Just think of the difference between the "arriving home" greeting of a small terrier and of a large hound: the former is likely to sound high-pitched ("yappy" to the non-fan); the latter will sound deeper and possibly slower, with fewer repeats, too.

HOME ALONE, OR STRANGER DANGER?

Even if some barks can be hard for humans to read easily, dogs seem to be able to tell what other dogs are barking about. Experiments in which recordings of the barks of one set of dogs in a variety of situations were played to another set of dogs have shown that the latter react differently, depending on the bark they hear.

For example, dogs listening to the repetitive "home alone" barking of others had little response; the same dogs, though, when played the bark made by a dog who had heard a stranger approaching outside, listened carefully, apparently paying much closer attention.

One study into dog talk, carried out in 2010 at Eötvös Loránd University, proved that dogs can tell how big another dog is by hearing its growl. Dogs were seated, one by one, in front of a screen that displayed an image of a large dog on the left and a small dog on the right, and were then played a series of growls (recorded from dogs guarding food) from either large or small dogs. When a large-dog growl was played, the study dogs looked at the picture of the large dog; when a small-dog growl was played, they looked at the smaller one. The researchers deduced that dogs knew the size of the threat behind the growl: "When growling," one said, "dogs don't lie about their size."

CLASSIC BARKS

While it's risky to generalize too broadly, if you compare a single dog's bark (either your own pet or one you know well) to the following guidelines, you'll probably find that the definitions fit the scenario the dog is barking in fairly closely.

Number of barks: Fast non-stop barking, quick repetition
Pitch: Mid-range
Message: I'm sounding the alarm because something or someone unfamiliar is approaching.

Number of barks: Barks grouped in repetitions of three to four, with pauses between groups
Pitch: Mid-range
Message: Something of interest is happening; this is to alert rather than to alarm.

Number of barks: One or two
Pitch: Rising, from mid- to high-range
Message: "Hello" bark; the dog is greeting another familiar dog or person.

Number of barks: Single barks, with pauses between each one
Pitch: Mid-range
Message: The "home alone" or "I'm here" bark; the dog is confined alone.

Number of barks: Single bark
Pitch: High-range
Message: Surprise; something unexpected is happening.

Number of barks: Rat-a-tat "a-ruff" stuttering bark
Pitch: Mid-range
Message: This is usually issued as a play invitation to another dog, often in combination with a play bow (front paws flat on the ground, rump in air).

Number of barks: Single bark
Pitch: Rising, from mid- to high-range
Message: Anticipatory bark; it is often heard during a play pause, either with another dog or with a person when playing football, fetch, etc.

CHAPTER 5: A DOG'S SENSES—TOUCH AND TASTE

After the superpower qualities of a dog's hearing, smell, and sight, their gifts in the areas of touch and taste may seem like a bit of an anticlimax. Nevertheless, there are still intriguing facts you probably didn't know about both senses. Who knew, for example, that dogs have special taste buds dedicated to water, or that they sweat from their pads when they're stressed? Knowing more about these senses will answer many questions about how dogs work.

FEELING THEIR SURROUNDINGS

Touch and smell are the two senses a puppy uses most from birth. Long before his eyes open or his hearing kicks in, a puppy will have smelled his mother, will have been licked and cleaned by her, and will have squirmed his way between his brothers and sisters to feed. And while the degree may vary from dog to dog, all dogs are highly touch-sensitive.

FROM HEAD TO TOE

Dogs have plenty of nerve endings all over their bodies, particularly down their spines, and despite their deceptively furry packaging, also have much thinner skin than humans. Their whiskers, called vibrissae, sit not just around the muzzle but also above the eyes and under the chin, and they are set three times deeper into the skin than normal hairs. Whiskers are sensitive to changes in airflow around the dog's face, and super-sensitive to touch, giving him an enhanced sense of the space around his head (this is useful for squeezing through tight spaces), as well as advance warning of an approaching hand or other object.

· ·

Dogs' paws are also arranged to give them the most information possible about the terrain they're on, while being tough enough to navigate rough ground. A dog has five pads on his back paws—the four smaller, or digital pads, and the larger metacarpal pad behind them—and six on his front paws, which have the same arrangement, plus an extra, carpal, pad located higher up the leg, near his "wrist." All the pads are well insulated with fat and have five layers of skin, which gives a thick, tough finish. And the carpal pad on the front feet acts as a "stopper" when a dog is going at speed, making it easier for him either to change direction or to skid to a halt.

· ·

The paw pads have one other less obvious feature: they sweat. Dogs famously can't sweat from their skin; that's why they pant on a hot day, in order to lower their body temperature in the only way they can. But they can and do sweat from their paw pads, and they do this not only in excessive heat, but also when they're highly stressed. If you see damp paw prints and it's not a hot day, you're looking at a nervous dog. Scientists have theorized that pad-sweating under stress may have a practical purpose; according to the fight-or-flight principle, if a dog needs to make a fast getaway, the dampened skin on his pads may give him extra traction when running.

TOUCHING DOGS

One of the most appealing things about dogs is how happy most are to be cuddled and petted; they're well known to be excellent stress-relievers, so much so that a US study in 2015 found that having a family dog was a key factor in reduced stress levels in children. Dogs are so keen to interact with us, in fact, that most people give comparatively little thought to how they touch their dog. And that's a pity, because while most dogs will put up with being touched in ways they don't like, it's easy enough to avoid when you know the whys and wherefores.

Humans are classified as members of the great ape subgroup of the hominids. And when it comes to touching other people, we exhibit typical great ape behavior: we love to put our arms around other people's shoulders and to hug, and we're also happy to touch each others faces with our hands, patting and stroking. And we tend to touch our dogs in similar ways. But dogs aren't apes, they're canidae, and they don't have the same preferences at all.

WHAT DOGS DO AND DON'T LIKE

Of course, different dogs like different things, but here are some touches that the majority of dogs enjoy. Rather than patting a dog on his head or along the top of his back, smooth, repetitive stroking along his sides is often appreciated. And many dogs like their cheeks to be stroked, along the bone under the eyes. Any touch that visibly relaxes a dog is doing it right, and if he rolls over for a belly rub (the ultimate canine compliment, showing both appreciation and trust), you'll know you've hit the spot.

Dogs usually hate being approached from above their heads, so the traditional pat of a dog on the head is the number one touch to avoid; they can't see the advancing hand, and so the sudden impact on the head, even if it isn't hard, appears threatening. A close second is putting an arm around a dog's shoulders; canids don't have a hug in their body language repertoire, and the only canine gesture remotely similar to a hug is the one in which another dog puts its body and paws up on your shoulders, which is a power play, and unless both parties understand each other very well, not likely to be a welcome one. A third way most dogs don't like to be touched is on their paws. Again, touching each other's paws isn't a common dog-to-dog gesture and seems to make dogs feel uncomfortably restrained. Plus, it may, for some dogs, have unwelcome associations with nail-clipping, which almost all dislike.

"HE LOVES TO BE PATTED!"

Maybe your dog has been patted on the head and hugged for years. Even if you're convinced he loves it, look carefully at his body language the next time you do it. Plenty of well-raised dogs wouldn't dream of growling at you, or even walking away, but you may find that he's really submitting to your odd hugging behavior, rather than actively enjoying it.

THE OXYTOCIN FACTOR

It's been known for a long time that one of the reasons we enjoy interacting with our dogs is that it raises our levels of the hormone oxytocin, also known as the feel-good hormone. Exclusive to mammals, its levels tend to rise when we're engaged in activities we enjoy and find rewarding, and when our oxytocin levels increase, so does our sense of well-being. High oxytocin levels make the world seem a better place, and they can also work on a loop, because the more oxytocin is released, the better we feel, and the more likely we are to engage in activities that will continue the feeling. A dog being petted and enjoying it will also see a raise in his oxytocin levels, so the benefits are mutual. And in 2016, research was published in the journal *Science* showing that when dogs and their owners were looking into each other's eyes from across a room, both could experience a raise in oxytocin levels.

GOAT MEETS DOG

One experiment undertaken for the BBC in the UK looked at whether two different nonhuman species can mutually raise oxytocin levels, and effectively form a friendship. At a multiple-species animal refuge in Arkansas, oxytocin levels were measured both before and after interaction between two animals of different species. The most striking result was when a small terrier and a goat, already friendly, were allowed to play together. After the play session, the goat's oxytocin levels were raised by a staggering 210 percent—as the researcher put it, it was as if the goat was in love with the dog. Sadly, if it was love, it was unrequited; the dog's levels were up by only 48 percent. He seemed to want to be just friends.

DID YOU KNOW. . .

Cross-species "friendships" are sometimes encouraged among captive animals. Keepers at the San Diego Zoo, for example, have long maintained a tradition of introducing cheetah cubs to puppies at a very young age. The dogs seem to have a stabilizing effect on the wild cats, calming their behavior and enabling the zoo to use the adult cheetahs to participate in their Animal Ambassadors program at public events.

TASTE

Puppies are born with a semi-developed sense of taste that matures over the first couple of weeks of life. Like humans, dogs are omnivores. Although their preferred wild diet would originally have been primarily meat, they can and will eat quite a broad range of foods. Like humans, they have receptors for sour, sweet, salty, and bitter tastes, in taste buds located on the top of their tongues and, to a lesser extent, on the roof and at the back of their mouths, and also in the throat. Compared with humans, however, dogs have far fewer taste buds—just 1,700, compared with the human total of 9,000.

In a highly developed human environment, it can seem as though the function of taste is to allow us to choose those foods that are most delicious to us from the wide range available. But millions of years ago, the original use for a sense of taste was to enable an animal to tell if something was edible at all, and if it would meet their nutritional needs to help them survive. They had to choose from a wide variety of substances as "food," and while some would nourish them, others might be poisonous, and the keener the sense of taste they had, the less likely they were to make mistakes. Something that tasted disgusting was unlikely to be a good choice.

The more complex the diet, the more taste buds were needed. Although dogs have less than a quarter of the human total, they still far outnumber those of cats, who come in with just 400 (cats, unlike dogs, are true carnivores).

TASTE SPECIALISTS

As well as the salty/sweet/sour/bitter combinations, dogs have some receptors that aren't found in humans. One set is dedicated to the tastes found in animal protein, specifically meat. Within meat, it seems likely that dogs can taste a wider range of flavors than we can. They also have taste buds dedicated to water (see page 88). Their salt receptors are present, but are weak compared to those found in humans.

The receptors for the different flavors are mainly grouped on different parts of the tongue—sour and salty to the sides, bitter at the back, and sweet mostly at the front, with water-sensitive receptors at the very front.

DID YOU KNOW. . .

Despite the fact that dogs' acid stomach linings generally give them a higher tolerance than humans for food that is definitely past its best, there are plenty of specific foodstuffs that can harm them. Most owners know that their pets shouldn't ever be given chocolate, but fewer are aware that dogs should not be given grapes, raisins, macadamia nuts, or anything containing the artificial sweetener xylitol, which can fatally lower a dog's insulin levels.

WHAT DOGS ENJOY

If you've watched a hungry dog eat, you will have noticed that he doesn't seem to savor his food; he's more likely to gulp it down as fast as he can than to stop and savor each mouthful. So does he really taste it at all, or, having established, with an initial sniff and a mouthful or two, that it isn't actually poisonous, is he simply filling his belly as fast as he can?

It's true that most dogs don't linger over their meals, but this doesn't mean they're not tasting the food. The most likely reason for your dog bolting his food is his ancestry: he comes from competitive predators, and no dog who lingered over a kill for long could expect an uninterrupted, or uncontested, meal. In studies, dogs have also been found to tend to prefer food that is both moist and warm, reflecting the qualities of a fresh prey kill.

EAT YOUR GREENS—AND FRUIT

Your pet may not get a lot of sweet food, but he has taste buds that detect sweetness. The substance they mainly respond to is furaneol, a natural compound found in a number of foods, including strawberries and raspberries, as well as tomatoes and buckwheat. It's conceivable that wild berries formed part of early dogs' foraged diet. Many dogs enjoy apples and carrots, both of which will appeal to the sweet area of their palates.

HOW MANY TASTE BUDS?

There's a huge variety in the number of taste buds found in different animal species. Most birds have very few (chickens, for example, have only around twenty-five). Carnivores have more, and herbivores more still—cows have an incredible 25,000 taste buds—probably because many herbivores have evolved to eat a diet based on a wide variety of different plant species and they need to be given taste clues as to whether or not a specific plant may be toxic (nature's way of warning of toxicity tends to be a bitter taste). And which animal has the greatest number of taste buds, and therefore the most refined palate? Hats off to the catfish, a bottom-feeder that lives in exceptionally muddy water, where it can't see much at all. To compensate, a large catfish may have as many as 175,000 taste buds, not only in its whiskery mouth but spread all over its body.

THE TASTE OF WATER

You may notice that your dog often spurns the clean tap water in his bowl at home, instead choosing to lap from the dirtiest puddle he can find outdoors. When you learn that he has some special taste buds on the end of his tongue that are adapted to the taste of water—taste buds that humans lack—this common habit seems even odder. What's the appeal of the puddle? And why does he need taste buds for water anyway?

Although dogs do have salt receptors among their taste buds, these are comparatively weak, and much weaker than the equivalent receptors in humans. It's thought that this is because dogs' naturally meat-heavy diet was high in salt (meat is a relatively salty substance), so they had less need to develop receptors that could help identify sources of salt. Their dietary need for salt was likely to have been met by what they ate anyway. But high salt levels can mean more urination, and ultimately dehydration, so if there's a danger of a dog's body having too much salt, he needs to drink more. The water receptors on his tongue are therefore an important tool in his efforts to source safe drinking water.

And your dog's taste for drinking from puddles? This may be a question of the "clean" water in his bowl having a taste he doesn't like, rather than the puddle having a taste that he does. Straight-from-the-tap drinking water that, to us, has no specific taste, may well taste unpleasantly "chemical" and artificial to our dogs.

HOW A DOG DRINKS

Dogs are loud and messy drinkers, and the way they take water in looks complicated to humans (and is in any case hard to see clearly when the dog is vigorously lapping). Slow-motion video of a dog drinking makes clear, however, that his method is actually efficient, and he manages to get more water into his mouth than might appear to be the case.

Here's how it works: first the tongue curls backward, then its tip is dipped into the water (the water-sensitive receptors are located just where a dog's tongue will first touch the water's surface). The length of the tongue follows. With the initial backward movement, the tongue has now formed an open-ended bag, which, as the tongue moves deeper under the surface, fills with water. As the dog pulls his tongue back into his mouth, a large amount of the water is pulled back with it on its underside. As soon as his tongue is back in his mouth, the dog shuts it, capturing most of the water, and the residue falls on the ground. As he swallows, he opens his mouth for the next lap.

A DOG'S DIGESTION

When dogs bolt their food, they're eating in a natural way. Dogs have forty-two teeth (ten more than the average human), which are designed to hold and tear prey and, when the prey is dead, to pull the meat and skin from the bone and to bite up the bone and grind it into swallowable pieces. They can't move their jaws sideways, only up and down. Unlike humans, they don't chew their food for prolonged periods. Instead, as soon as their food is in manageable lumps, they swallow it.

Weight-for-weight, dogs are able to eat a lot more than humans in a single meal—around five percent of their body weight in one go, although a human-controlled diet means that modern pets will rarely be given this chance. The eat-till-you-burst capacity reflects the life of dogs in the wild, where a dog would be more likely to make a kill, eat to repletion, then go for a few days without food.

People have enzymes in their mouths that begin the digestion process while they are still chewing. Dogs don't—a dog's digestive enzymes are produced by his pancreas and in his stomach, and the latter is an extremely acid environment, with a pH somewhere between 1 and 2 (by comparison, human stomach acid has a pH of around 5). Once the pieces of roughly bitten-up food reach the dog's stomach, they take around four to six hours to digest.

WHAT YOUR DOG EATS

Of course, the timing of the digestive process depends on what your dog was eating in the first place. If he has eaten raw meat and bone, the digestion process is faster (and, some think, closer to the natural "norm"); if he has a tinned food or dry diet, digestion may take a few hours longer. Dogs' diets of today are vastly more varied than they were in the past— from highly processed foods to raw meat and BARF diets (which feature foods that dogs would be eating in an undomesticated, wild state), and their digestions are equipped to deal with the more challenging end of the scale.

CATCHING YOUR OWN

Some recent research seems to show that dogs are better at tracking and catching animals they have already eaten than those they haven't. Game dogs were given meals of the birds they would later have to scent and collect, and this increased their success retrieving the birds later on. The tentative scientific explanation for this was that if, for example, a dog was fed pheasant, molecules from the meal entered his bloodstream and sharpened his scent for the trail.

CHAPTER 6: A SIXTH SENSE?

To most dog owners, their dogs seem strongly empathetic; often, they appear not only to know how you feel, but actually to feel like you feel, too. And with a bond as strong as that, it's hardly surprising that many people believe that dogs have a sixth sense, a sensibility that isn't altogether explicable in normal sensory terms. This chapter looks at some of the unexplained phenomena, whereby dogs seem to "just know," along with the science behind how this may be possible.

EXTRASENSORY SKILLS?

All kinds of extrasensory abilities are attributed to dogs, from being able to "sign" the answers to questions put by their owners to "just knowing" when those owners are coming home. There's a perennial debate between those who are happy to believe that dogs have extrasensory or even psychic powers, and scientists looking for hard proof. The plus side is that this has led to a number of intriguing experiments aimed at establishing just how it is that dogs seem to know what they know.

One of the most common situations cited is that of a dog who can anticipate, long before a car might be heard in the drive, when their owner is going to get home. Examples are given of dogs suddenly going to the window, or otherwise acting on full alert with no apparent sign, in human terms, at least, of an imminent arrival, and then a couple of minutes later the owner arrives. There have been various tests exploring this phenomenon, many predicated on a likely combination of the dog's supercharged sense of hearing, allied with owners who wanted their dogs to have some kind of superpower, so were unwittingly skewing results in favor of it.

An intriguingly different theory was advanced and tested by Alexandra Horowitz, who runs the Dog Cognition Lab at Barnard College in New York. She specializes in studying how dogs' sense of smell works and wanted to see if the dog's scenting ability might actually be involved, rather than magical powers of prediction. Could it be, she wondered, that rather than the dog magically hearing his owner from a greater distance and through more obstacles than was believed possible, he was instead conducting a countdown of the unique scent molecules that his owner had left behind when he departed in the morning, and "alerting" when the scent had faded to a certain point? We know that dogs have relatively accurate body clocks (a dog who is regularly fed at a certain time will almost invariably be able to judge when it's dinnertime and alert his owners, even when he's given no external signal to do so). So, perhaps the dog knew that his owner usually came back when his scent had diminished to a certain level.

The test she carried out involved a dog being left at home, as usual. After some hours, however, a freshly worn t-shirt belonging to his owner was clandestinely put into the house, boosting the familiar "owner scent," although the owner himself didn't return. The experiment seemed to prove her point; usually, when his person came back, the dog was standing to attention at the door, ready to greet. But on the day the owner's scent in the home was given a mid-day boost, the dog was still asleep when his owner returned.

CANINE INTELLECTUALS

On the question of canine geniuses that share their knowledge by "signing" their owners, the well-known US author and behaviorist Patricia McConnell shared a cautionary story from the experiences of Dan Estep and Suzanne Hetts of Animal Behavior Associates in Colorado. They had been asked to evaluate a dog named Sheba, whose owner claimed that she knew, and could demonstrate, a wide range of general knowledge. She answered questions on all sorts of subjects, either by tapping her owner's hand with her paw, to signify yes or no, or pawing multiple times to answer more complicated queries. Her owner was convinced she knew the answers from her fund of general knowledge, in the same way that a person would.

In controlled tests, though, there was an immediate drawback: Sheba couldn't answer questions if she couldn't see her owner, and she couldn't answer, either, if she was asked a question to which he didn't know the answer himself. The testers were convinced that he wasn't cuing Sheba deliberately, so how was she answering correctly?

The test couldn't be completed because the author, offended, withdrew from the study when Sheba's "real" knowledge was questioned. It seemed certain that she was gauging the correct replies from unconscious cues he was giving her, whether by the touch of his hand or the expression on his face. A group of trainers and behaviorists watched videos of the tests without finding the answer, but dogs are known experts in the tiniest shifts in body language, and it seems likely that Sheba was an unusually skilled practitioner of this established canine gift.

Both these stories support most canine experts' belief that there is plenty about dogs' special abilities still to be uncovered, and that dogs' senses are remarkable in their own right. They don't need to have additional psychic or extrasensory skills to astonish a human audience.

DOGS THAT HELP

Although the range of official jobs for which dogs are employed has expanded hugely over the last forty or so years, the skills that these jobs require were part of a dog's skillset long before. Humans have simply applied them in varying contexts as they have learned more about canine skills.

HOW DID THEY KNOW?

Dogs have usually been the first to alert people as to their suitability for a particular role. The first guide dog program, back in 1916, came about because a German doctor, Gerhard Stalling, needing to leave a blind patient alone for a while, left his dog with him for company and noticed on his return that dog and patient had formed an instinctive bond, the dog seeming to have a sense that the patient needed help. In the same way, the idea that dogs could be trained to be the "ears" for deaf people arose in the 1970s from cases in which the untrained pets of the deaf adapted naturally to the disability of their owners and learned to make visual signs, rather than noises, to gain attention.

Detection dogs, whether they're detecting for diseases or dynamite, have a rather more complex history. The skills their trainers are calling on are the same as those used historically for tracker dogs, so are not new, but a bomb or drug detection dog needs a very high hit rate, so extended training around an extremely specific and limited range of smells is necessary to make them reliable. The principle is simple—mark the smell and earn a reward—but a number of variables must be taken into account (for example, a hungry dog will lose concentration, but one that's just been fed may lose accuracy because the food smells are lingering in his nose). Dogs training to sniff out cancer and other diseases have an even harder job, because they are working with living people, each of whom will have his or her unique cocktail of complicated smells through which to navigate. And it's the area of disease detection in which researchers are feeling their path. It seems certain that dogs can do the job, but humans are still learning the best way to use them.

THE ODD CASE OF THE BEDBUG DOGS

Sometimes, a dog's nose can be too sensitive. One rare case of canine failure arose when an epidemic of bedbugs afflicted New York in 2010. A number of companies boasting pest-sniffing dogs rose up to meet the demand of the city's disgusted residents, but the failure rate seemed unusually high. Dogs would indicate bedbugs in most apartments in a block, only for pest controllers, following them in, to find nothing to exterminate. Why did the dogs in this case prove so unreliable? The likeliest answer seems to be that the dogs' noses were smelling across a much larger area than a single cramped New York apartment, and detecting bugs that were actually several apartments away.

JUST BEING THERE

One aspect of human–dog interaction that's attracting increasing amounts of research is an unconscious feel-good factor that humans enjoy when around dogs. This isn't the oxytocin fix we get from petting our dogs; it seems that the mere presence of dogs may have a positive effect on how we behave socially.

Every dog owner knows that just walking your dog can improve your social life. But a study carried out at Central Michigan University in 2012 found that the positive effects of dogs on people might be much less obvious than we'd otherwise suspect.

DOGS HELP PEOPLE BOND BETTER

The experiment put together small groups of workers to do simple but cooperative and creative tasks. Half the groups had a pet dog in the room while they were working; the other half didn't. When the jobs were completed, participants were asked about how well they felt the group had worked together, and how well they had worked with individuals.

The results? Those groups that had had a dog "working" with them reported a higher degree of helpfulness and closer work relationships with their coworkers than the groups without. They bonded strongly and trusted the other people in the group more.

The groups were also filmed while working together and the videos watched back by independent observers. The footage didn't reveal which groups had a dog and which did not, but the independent witnesses reported observing more instances of positive, cooperative behavior and better teamwork in the former groups. They also selected the with-dog teams as ranking higher in apparent enthusiasm and alertness.

The groups' success in the tasks they worked on didn't seem to be affected by whether or not there was a dog in the room: it was the social interaction and the bonding over work that reflected the difference.

The scientists at Michigan found the results intriguing. This was the first study of its kind, in that it didn't call for the dog to do anything—the groups weren't encouraged to notice the dog or to interact with it—it was simply there. The experiment has raised the idea that a canine presence may do our emotional settings good, and has provoked other studies looking at what might cause the effect. Watch this space; perhaps the time will come when dogs will actually be prescribed for our well-being in the workplace!

DID YOU KNOW. . .

Over the last decade, the benefits of having pets in the workplace have been acknowledged by some major businesses. Google's code of conduct contains a clause relating to animals at work that states: "Google's affection for our canine friends is an integral facet of our corporate culture." The success of bring-your-dog-to-work schemes prompted one forward-looking CEO at 2016's World Economic Forum at Davos to suggest that it could prove to be a model for employees who needed in-office care, not only for their pets, but for aging relatives too.

NEW AND FUTURE ROLES FOR DOGS

Dogs have been helping hunters and farmers for centuries, but the idea that a dog might offer a person one-to-one assistance based on behaviors developed specifically for that purpose is not new. The idea of guide dogs for the blind seems to have originated in 18th-century France, and the first formal training school for guide dogs opened in 1916. Dogs were also first used as scouts during the First World War, warning of enemy approaches before soldiers could hear or see them.

So these newer roles for dogs have come a huge distance in just a century. Today, dogs are trained in multiple disciplines, as guide dogs and hearing dogs, and dogs that can sniff out everything from cancerous tumors to explosives. There are even emotional support dogs who can help people on the autism spectrum, seizure-alert dogs who can anticipate when an epileptic is going to have a fit or a diabetic is headed for a dangerous sugar spike, and dogs who can help those suffering from post-traumatic stress. So what is the future likely to bring when it comes to new work for dogs?

NEW JOBS FOR DOGS

New areas where dogs' natural skills can be more useful than the most sophisticated machine, and new places where dogs can practice already established careers, include:

Conservation worker

Dogs are being used to track rare and endangered species in the wild— for example, they've been used to detect signs of their endangered fellow species, the African wild dog, shown opposite. They can cover a lot of ground and detect the scent of species reliably in cases where the only previous options were to use traps to establish the presence of rare animals.

Invasive species detector

Dogs can trace plant and animal species that shouldn't be there, and that may pose a threat to indigenous flora and fauna, long before their presence is evident to humans. Catching invaders at an early stage makes it easier to deal with them before they become a serious problem.

Grief counselor

Many owners might say that dogs have always done this job. However, it's only recently that they've been co-opted by funeral directors and grief therapists as in-house help, to provide silent comfort.

Prison therapist

Helping with stable work has been part of jail rehabilitation programs all over the world; working with horses has been found to help prisoners work cooperatively and to aid in anger management. But it's expensive, and new enterprises that aim to do the same sort of work with shelter dogs are more affordable and seem to offer many of the same benefits.

In the 1990s, the American writer on leadership Warren Bennis made a comic prediction. "The factory of the future will only have two employees," he said, "a man and a dog. The man will be there to feed the dog. The dog will be there to keep the man from touching the equipment." He may have anticipated the balance correctly, but it seems likely that working dogs in the future will have more rewarding jobs than that.

SECTION TWO
EXPLORING WHAT YOUR DOG KNOWS

After a long period in the research wilderness the domestic dog is the current global star of studies in cognition and intelligence. In the first quarter of the 21st century, we've become fascinated by the gaps in our knowledge of this completely familiar species. Dogs have lived alongside us for centuries, yet it's only recently that we've begun to wonder what life is like for them, and whether they think and feel all the things we assume them to feel. Do they love us? Do they ever feel embarrassed? Can they tell lies? What do they really think about humans? And as our curiosity has grown, so we focus less on how we can make our dogs understand us, and more on what we can learn about, and from, them.

This section looks at how we know what we know about dogs, and introduces some new and imaginative ways in which you can interact with them.

CHAPTER 7: CANINE COGNITION

When it comes to studying the workings of another mammal, it seems a no-brainer that humans would choose dogs. Side-by-side companions for millennia, the two species seem to have a natural chemistry and a mutual affection. Yet surprisingly, other primates were the go-to species for in-depth research for most of the 20th century, and it's only in the last thirty or so years that scientists have focused on dogs for in-depth species-specific research. This chapter looks at how we know what we know about dogs.

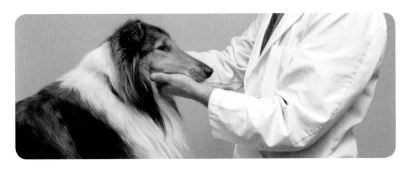

EARLY DOG STUDIES

As in so many other areas of biology and science, the story of modern dog studies begins with Charles Darwin. In his last book, *The Expression of the Emotions in Man and Animals*, published in 1872—a study which posited that animals and people felt emotion in a similar way—he looked at dogs' body language and embarked on an analysis of the emotions he believed they felt. Engravings of Polly, one of his terriers, were used to illustrate the postures and facial expressions he described. Although much of what he wrote still makes good sense today, his canine studies were always within a wider, multi-species context.

Ivan Pavlov, a Russian physiologist whose experimental work on digestion in the 1890s led him, almost accidentally, to discover that dogs could learn to connect one thing with another and react to it, and thus to develop the theory of classical conditioning, was nevertheless, like Darwin, studying dogs within a broader context, rather than focusing his research solely on them.

And despite Pavlov and Darwin's work, dogs were far from the most popular research subjects for major studies through most of the 20th century. Scientists believed that domestication made them less rather than more valuable to study, feeling that, since dogs were so familiar to people, it would be impossible to get unbiased results. Instead, they concentrated on animals, such as dolphins and chimpanzees, which were judged to have their original, natural thinking processes intact. Gradually, at the end of the century, both the style and the focus of studies changed, but not before going through an almost universally popular scientific phase known as behaviorism. Behaviorism would absorb many scientists and their work through the mid-20th century, until it began finally to fall out of favor in the late 1960s.

DID YOU KNOW. . .

Darwin not only studied dogs but was also an enthusiastic pet owner. At Cambridge University he owned a pointer, Dash, and in later life he owned a whole range of dogs, including a number of terriers, a Scottish deerhound, and a Pomeranian.

APE TO HUMAN, WOLF TO DOG?

The very quality that used to disqualify dogs from scientific research—their domesticated state—has become an active asset in studies today. One theory proposes that the gradual evolution of man from ape may be mirrored in the evolution of domestic dog from wolf. What if, instead of dogs being scientifically judged as somehow "inferior" to wolves by virtue of their tame status, they are actually a logical evolutionary progression, just as humans consider themselves to be?

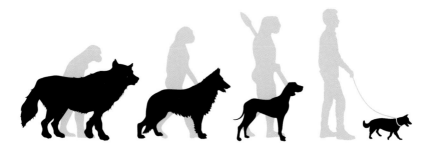

BEHAVIORISM VERSUS COGNITION

Behaviorism, or, by its full name, behavioral psychology, was one of the most influential movements in science between the 1920s and the 1960s. Its focus lay on how living things behave, without going into the whys and wherefores of that behavior.

It proposed that humans (and animals) are born as blank slates, that they are shaped entirely by their environment and their responses to it, and it took no account of the internal thoughts or the emotional life of people or animals. American psychologist B. F. Skinner, its leading theorist and practitioner in the mid-20th century, and an enthusiast for Pavlov's experiments, was the first to use the term "operant conditioning." This theory was based on the idea that particular sorts of behavior can be changed by a pattern of rewards and punishments, the former to reinforce them and the latter to weaken them. Skinner believed that human society could be run on behaviorist principles, and at its height behaviorism influenced everything from educational theory to animal studies and even the treatment of mental illness.

STRAIGHTFORWARD AND LIMITED

Behaviorism held that there were limits to what anyone could know or find out about how any mind, be it a person, dog, or dolphin, worked. It proved possible to shape behavior to a remarkable degree in animals, and Skinner conducted a number of experiments in which he trained animals to do extraordinary things. In 1950 he famously trained a pair of pigeons to play ping-pong through a laborious process comprising numerous stages. But over time, behaviorism fell out of fashion because there were too many things that it didn't explain, and while many of its theories about shaping behavior "worked" in a practical sense, its approach was too hidebound to be applied to factors such as environmental adaptability and intelligence.

DID YOU KNOW. . .
If you've ever considered consulting a professional about a behavioral problem with your pet, be aware that the term "behaviorist" can be used very loosely by practitioners in the US and UK, and doesn't necessarily denote specialist training. In the US, the qualification to look for is CAAB (Certified Applied Animal Behaviorist), which requires rigorous training.

THE RISE OF COGNITION

More adventurous thinkers wanted to look at theories that embraced the behavior and the mental life of both animals and people, and it was the kickback against behaviorism that caused the rise of cognitive science. Today, most scientists would concede that behaviorism can have its uses—clicker training, for example, which is hugely popular among dog owners, employs classic shaping behavior—but it's seen as too limited to fill in the whole picture.

And what does this have to do with dogs? The questioning of behaviorism opened the door to a much freer approach to cognition, which today looks at how the mind works in all kinds of ways and in all kinds of animals. And most recently, the natural study partner in such research has proved to be the domestic dog.

IS YOUR DOG PSYCHIC?

Of course, no single theory, scientific or otherwise, enjoys univeral support. One interesting but highly controversial contemporary theorist is Rupert Sheldrake, the author of the book *Dogs That Know When Their Authors Are Coming Home.*

Sheldrake, a biologist and writer, developed a concept called morphic resonance, which he believes accounts for many previously inexplicable phenomena, such as the way in which animals seem able to predict earthquakes and tsunamis. Morphic resonance, a concept that lies far outside mainstream thinking, is the idea that the natural world holds inherent memories that are passed down through living things—"things are as they are because they were as they were." *Dogs That Know…* came out in 1999, by which time Sheldrake had already published several books putting forward his world picture. Among this book's arguments was the proposal that telepathy was possible between humans and animals, and, as the title suggested, Sheldrake used studies with dogs that "just knew" when their owners were coming home, independent of external clues, to prove his point. Unlike Alexandra Horowitz, who, some years later, would argue that a dog's sense of smell might account for it "just knowing" (see page 59), Sheldrake was convinced that interspecies telepathy was the explanation.

THE CASE OF JAYTEE

Sheldrake's best-known experiments were conducted on a dog called Jaytee and her owner. In these, the dog was filmed constantly when her owner was out. The amount of time she spent at the window, looking out for her owner, was monitored according to whether or not her owner was actually on her way home. The times at which the owner traveled home varied, as did the way she traveled. Sheldrake believed that it was the telepathic connection between dog and owner that led Jaytee to watch at the window; other scientists argued that the experiment was flawed. The arguments have flowed to and fro without resolution. Was Jaytee psychic? The case remains unproven.

HOW DO LOST DOGS FIND THEIR WAY HOME?

Sheldrake's theories take their place in the field of unusual and unexplained dog behavior alongside many others. New studies are constantly seeking to explain why dogs do what they do, when no known scientific theory can offer a satisfactory explanation. One of the questions that perennially fascinates owners and scientists alike, and invariably makes for a popular press story, is how on earth lost dogs can make their way home, sometimes across vast distances and traveling unfamiliar routes, in order to reunite with their owners. One of the earliest recorded cases of this phenomenon was that of Bobbie the collie who, in 1923, found his way from Indiana, where he'd become separated from his family while on holiday, back home to Oregon, a journey of over 2,500 miles—one that he accomplished in around six months. Just a year later he starred in a film of his adventures, but back in the 1920s no one could offer any scientifically credible answer to how he might have made the trip. It seemed truly miraculous, and skeptics questioned whether it was even the same dog that had returned.

Other such stories have cropped up every so often ever since; as recently as 2016, the tale of a dog called Pero hit the headlines in Britain. Pero, a sheepdog, took two weeks to make the journey from Cumbria, northern England, back to his home in Aberystwyth, Wales. At around 250 miles, his journey was a mere tenth of the length of Bobbie's, but it was still impressive, and in the age of the microchip, it was easy enough to prove that he was the same dog. But there were still plenty of questions as to how he had done it.

After all, he'd traveled to Cumbria by car, so it wasn't a case of retracing the route he'd walked before (a feat which would have been remarkable enough in itself). And although we know just how extraordinary the canine sense of smell is, it seems unlikely that it could guide a dog hundreds of miles, let alone, as in the case of Bobbie, thousands.

DO DOGS HAVE AN INTERNAL COMPASS?

Scientists have tried experiments to investigate whether or not dogs have a sensitivity to the Earth's magnetic field, enabling them to navigate using a kind of internal GPS. Others have pointed to the fact that other species undertake immense journeys in the form of annual migration, which are at least as remarkable as some of the one-off journeys of individual animals. Many species of bird and whale, for example, navigate precise journeys of thousands of miles every year.

The latest discovery is that dogs have a light-sensitive molecule called cryptochrome 1 located in the cone cells of their retinas, which may enable them to "see" magnetic fields. The research is still at a fairly early stage, and it's not yet clear how animals use this ability, although in one experiment it was found that foxes seem to use it when hunting by orienting themselves along a northeast axis before pouncing on their prey, apparently because it enables them to target more accurately and therefore leads to a higher success rate in catching dinner. The next step for researchers will be to establish what the presence of the molecule signifies, and whether it's the tip of the iceberg when it comes to finding out quite how many additional sensory abilities dogs have that aren't yet explained or suspected. Can dogs navigate by means of an internal compass? We don't know, but it looks as though the question may be answered before too long.

DOGS: THE PERFECT SCIENCE SUBJECTS

When dogs were first proposed as subjects for cognitive research, they were a resoundingly unfashionable choice. In an article published in *Science* in 2009, Ádám Miklósi, now one of the foremost scientists working in canine cognition, went on record as having been stunned when, back in 1994, his director at Eötvös Loránd University proposed doing some research into dogs. "'My God, are you crazy?' That's what I thought, although I didn't say it," he remembered.

The prejudice against dogs was deep rooted, but was gradually overcome. Between the 1990s and the early 2000s, the research picture gradually transformed. Far from being scientific outcasts, dogs were fast becoming a top research species all over the world, with dog cognition labs opening in many universities.

CANINE COGNITION WINS OUT

Why have dogs become such popular subjects for study?

- They enjoy interacting with people, which makes them easy to work with.

- They're cheap subjects to study; most of the dogs used in cognitive research are pets who don't live in the lab.

- They're an infinite resource. Unlike some rarer species that have been popular subjects in the past, researchers always have more dogs to call on, and that's important when trying to achieve broad scientific proof of new discoveries.

- From being viewed as a drawback, their domesticated status is now seen as an advantage in social studies.

- The dog's genome was mapped by 2005, meaning that it should theoretically be possible to link specific genes with particular behaviors—a holy grail for many scientists.

CANINE AMBASSADORS

Dogs have another advantage: they have a massive fan club, with their popularity extending far beyond the lab. Dog lovers and owners enjoy reading about them and are enthusiastic about any confirmation of special gifts or intelligence that dogs may have. New discoveries about their social behavior, their ancestry, or the way in which they think are eagerly devoured by a general public who might be left cold by the same revelations made about, say, the cotton-top tamarin (a small monkey that is also a popular research subject). Using dogs gives research far more publicity and moves it firmly toward the mainstream. From being frankly aghast at the idea of using dogs in cognitive research, Dr. Miklósi went on to found the Family Dog Research Project, the first research group in the world, and today one of the largest, to look at the relationship between dogs and people.

THE IMITATION GAME

From behaviorism, which focuses on moderating and controlling behavior, to canine cognition, which looks at which behaviors come naturally and at different sorts of intelligence, is a long road. And the two fields can still sometimes overlap. They did when, in 2013, the news that dogs were able to imitate people hit the headlines.

In canine cognition terms, this was big news. Consistent, visible cross-species imitation hadn't been found since work done in the 1950s with a baby chimpanzee called Viki—and chimpanzees are, like humans, great apes. Keith and Catherine Hayes had intended to raise Viki experimentally and had invented a system called Do As I Do (DAID) to teach her to copy them. To imitate may be the sincerest form of flattery, but it's also complicated behavior in social terms. In 2006 the Hayes's system was revived in Budapest by an ethologist called József Topál, this time to teach a dog. By 2013, a large group of dogs had been taught DAID, and today it's a popular training system with how-to books available and plenty of press coverage.

HOW DOES DAID WORK?

To successfully imitate someone else's action, a dog needs to, first, know to pay attention to what's coming next, second, to watch it, and third to perform the action himself. At first it was thought that only exceptional dogs would manage all three, but over the next few years many dogs mastered the art of imitation and DAID has become a popular training aid. Numerous videos show dogs enthusiastically following their trainers in a whole sequence of activities, from pulling a toy along the floor to jumping in and out of a cardboard box. Velvet, the pet dog of Claudia Fugazza, one of DAID's best-known practitioners, now imitates her without being asked, even climbing into the bath after Fugazza has emptied it and "relaxing" there, just like her owner does.

WHAT'S THE SIGNIFICANCE?

In research, successful imitation implies memory in dogs (they have to remember the action to imitate it, and some dogs have remembered trainers' actions up to an hour later). In cognitive science, memory has strong links with self-awareness. Are dogs self-aware? That is, does a dog know that he is himself and therefore different from others around him? The traditional test for self-awareness, which has been passed by many great apes, dolphins, and a few other species, is to see whether or not an animal recognizes its reflection in a mirror. Dogs have always failed at this, but that may be more to do with the way they see than anything else.

HOW DOLPHINS SEE THEMSELVES

Animals being tested in a mirror for self-awareness first have marks put on their bodies—a dolphin's body might be painted with a black "X," say. The dolphin will pass the test if, on seeing the mark in their reflection, they twist around to look at it on their own body, or try to remove it, or move their body to study the mark from a different angle. A chimpanzee, given the same test, will feel for the mark on its body, and would also look at the marks on other chimps, if the study has marked more than one animal. Dogs show no such awareness of their reflected image. You might assume that humans would pass the mirror test easily, but they "grow into it," only showing self-awareness after the age of about eighteen months.

SMELLING YOURSELF

Thinking laterally, Alexandra Horowitz at Barnard College in New York devised an alternative to the mirror test, one based on smell. If an animal who looks in a mirror with self-awareness sees himself, she reasoned, then it ought to be possible to figure out whether dogs, who smell the world as much as they see it, could smell themselves and exhibit self-awareness in that way. She collected a number of pee samples from dogs and put tiny traces of different samples in canisters, then allowed individual dogs into a room that was empty apart from two canisters, one containing a minute sample of their own pee, and the other containing an equally tiny sample of something else—either another dog's pee or a tissue sample from another dog. Thirty-seven dogs were tested and all spent considerably more time smelling their own sample than the other ones on offer.

Does Horowitz's "smell mirror" test prove that dogs are self-aware? Not everyone agrees, but it seems to be a step in the right direction (and most dog owners are probably rooting for the self-awareness of their pets). Scientifically, the point isn't considered proved, and whether or not dogs possess self-awareness remains a hot topic in cognitive research.

CANINE COGNITION LABS: PET DOGS GO MAINSTREAM

Once pet dogs were established as interesting subjects for study, it was only a matter of time before their owners got involved. Dr. Brian Hare, who runs the Duke Canine Cognition Center at Duke University in North Carolina, was perhaps one of the first to point out that most owners, convinced they had their own canine genius at home, can't get him into the lab to be tested fast enough.

What's more, some programs being developed don't even require dog owners to bring their pets into the lab; highly structured tests and experiments with plenty of how-to advice, accompanied by detailed questionnaires, have created "citizen scientists," who will undertake the research work for free. In some studies, such as the Dognition Assessment (see below), they even pay for the privilege.

CANINE COGNITION GOES GLOBAL

Canine cognition labs are now found in universities all over the world. This list of just a handful, with the subjects they're researching, will give you an idea of the range of dog studies:

Canine Cognition Center, Yale University
How dogs' vision works; dogs and human social cues; canine choice; touchscreen work

Dog Cognition Centre, University of Portsmouth, UK
Human–dog communication; how dogs learn from humans and other dogs; what dogs know about themselves; dogs' understanding of their physical environment; dogs' facial expressions

Horowitz Dog Cognition Lab, New York
Dog–human play; olfactory discrimination of dogs; empirical investigation of anthropomorphism; use of attention and play signals in social play; intra-canid vocalizations

La Trobe University, Bendigo, Australia
Bonds between dogs and people; psychological and social benefits of service dogs; auditory signals that help dogs learn

The Family Dog Project, Eötvös Loránd University
Evolutionary and ethological foundations of the dog–human relationship

THE DOGNITION ASSESSMENT
With an advisory board that is a roll call of the big names in the canine research world and an altogether new approach to testing dogs, The Dognition Assessment, another brainchild of Dr. Brian Hare, may be a taste of things to come in canine research. It works like a mixture of research tool and crowdfunding project, whereby participants join up, pay a fee, and receive information on how to test their dogs, including a detailed questionnaire and instructions on how to carry out ten games or exercises with their dog, divided into five categories: empathy, communication, cunning, memory, and reasoning.

When owners complete the program and send off the results, they receive a personality "diagnosis" from a choice of nine profiles on their pet, characterizing him as a charmer, maverick, stargazer, socialite, and so on. The fees part-pay the research behind the project.

It's possible that in the future, research done at home and beamed back to the researchers will be the norm. Supporters of the system point to its efficiency in getting studies of many, many more subjects than could be taken in the lab, while detractors worry about the partiality of the owners undertaking the tests.

WHAT HAPPENS NEXT: THE FUTURE OF DOG STUDIES

Now that canine cognition studies are firmly established in the research world, what does the future hold? What might be discovered about dogs in the course of the next decade? Which directions will the new generation of scientists take? Here's a speculative look at what might be coming in the world of dog research.

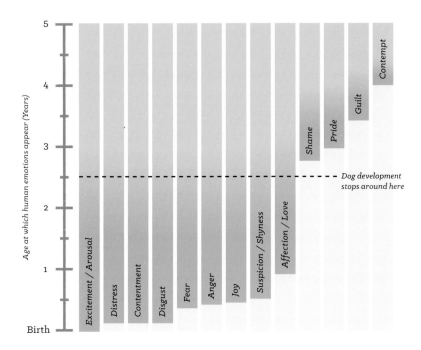

EMOTIONS

Back in the 17th century, the French philosopher René Descartes claimed that dogs had no feelings, that essentially they were insentient beings that happened to be alive. Over three centuries later, scientific opinion has moved light-years away from this view, and it seems likely that it will move even farther, as more work is done on canine emotions. The current position is that dogs can feel about the same spectrum of emotions as a human toddler—including happiness, anger, fear, and disgust, but not the more nuanced feelings that develop later in humans, such as guilt and shame (in particular, a number of experiments conclusively proved that dogs don't feel guilt, even if they do sometimes have "guilty" facial expressions). This is an area where there are still plenty of unanswered questions, though, and it's a likely target for future cognition studies.

NEW WAYS TO ASK THE QUESTION

Researchers who work with animals know that the problem they have to solve is often how to ask their questions in a way that will enable the animal to answer them. It's likely that in the future the ways in which scientists can "ask" dogs questions will focus on new technology, such as MRI and fMRI scanners. (MRI, magnetic resource imaging, is used to make brain scans, while fMRI, functional magnetic resource imaging, uses an MRI scanner but is set up to increase blood flow to active areas of the brain.) Successful attempts at training dogs to stay still for long enough to enable the machines to do their work make it likely that this technology will have a big part to play in the future.

MEMORY AND WHAT IT MEANS

Memory is likely to remain popular as a study subject. The DAID technique seemed to establish that dogs have longer memories than had been previously thought—prior to this, the estimate was of canine memory capacity of about two minutes—but it's still an area with plenty of gaps to be filled in.

CHAPTER 8: READ YOUR DOG

You know that he can't talk, and if you look at things from his point of view, you haven't got much of a sense of smell, so the preferred ways that your respective species communicate aren't open to either of you. But that needn't prevent you from picking up some pointers on how both your own and other dogs are feeling through body language. You've seen how dogs' senses work in earlier chapters; this chapter shows how their body language communicates with those around them, both human and canine.

UNDERSTANDING "DOG"

If you stand to one side in some open space and watch a group of dogs interacting, off-leash and without their humans looming in close to them, you may be surprised at quite how much is going on. Like a chatty group of humans, dogs are in constant communication.

They run up or approach more cautiously, sniff closely, step aside, make a big deal of doing a small pee, play bow to a prospective play partner, and plenty more. If your dog is comfortable mixing, take five minutes regularly to watch him interacting, and after just a week you'll find that not only will you start to recognize repeat behaviors, you'll also begin to separate out canine characters in much more detail than you might have previously thought possible.

There's always plenty going on in a mixed group of dogs. There are those dogs whose intentions are obvious, and others you have to watch more closely to see what's going on. There's the apparently impervious "guy walking into a bar" dog, who tries his social luck with every other dog in the area and who doesn't seem to notice, or at any rate take to heart, the fact that at least half the other dogs don't want to play with him. And then there's the shy dog, who seems happiest hanging around at the edges of activity and who will try a quick sniff of another dog's rear end only if the front end of the second dog seems fully occupied with something else. And then there are all the middle-grounders, milling around, sniffing often and openly, playing enthusiastic chase-me with any other dog who's willing, and occasionally standing aside to pee some information for another dog who seems interested.

HOW DO DOGS LEARN "DOG"?

How fluent dogs are with others depends on both nature and nurture. A puppy's natural personality plays a part; some dogs are seemingly born outgoing (and easygoing), while others have more inbuilt caution and are less happy about new experiences. How good their dog-to-dog social skills are can usually be explained by the amount of socialization a dog was given during the key development window (taken by most experts to be between four and sixteen weeks old) in puppyhood. Puppies socialized widely and successfully during this time tend to have good fluency with other dogs as adults, although character still counts—even the widest and most careful socialization probably won't turn a shy puppy into an extrovert. And breadth of socialization seems to count, too; studies have found that a puppy who has been brought up as a member of a family pack won't necessarily find that he has the dog skills to cope with a range of unfamiliar canines unless he also encountered a wider group during his development period. Once the development window is passed, a dog who hasn't been socialized (or hasn't been socialized enough) may still manage eventually to mix successfully with others, but it will probably never come quite so easily to him.

PLAY LIKE A DOG

Do dogs recognize signs that an animal of another species wants to play? One experiment encouraged owners to "play bow" to their dogs (stooped over, hands near the floor, bottom in air, finished with a wiggle), and found that the dogs seemed to "read" the classic "want-to-play?" signal, even though it wasn't being sent by another dog. Whether or not you want to try this with your own dog may depend on how self-conscious it makes you feel!

BODY TALK

If you were asked to say how someone is feeling without talking to them, you'd probably look at their face first, and then go on to check their body language to get the whole picture. You can follow the signals in the same way with dogs.

Dog behaviorists, used to situations where it really matters—for example, when assessing an aggressive dog—have learned to add up the pointers that tell you how a dog is feeling in nanoseconds. While you may never be quite as rapid, you can pick up a lot with a quick head-to-tail look, once you know what to look for. Here's a look at some places you can see tell-tale signs; the following pages will look at each in a bit more detail.

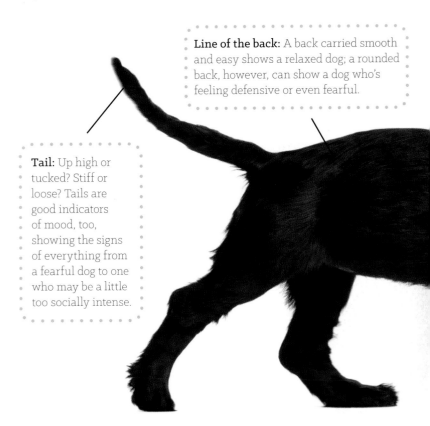

Line of the back: A back carried smooth and easy shows a relaxed dog; a rounded back, however, can show a dog who's feeling defensive or even fearful.

Tail: Up high or tucked? Stiff or loose? Tails are good indicators of mood, too, showing the signs of everything from a fearful dog to one who may be a little too socially intense.

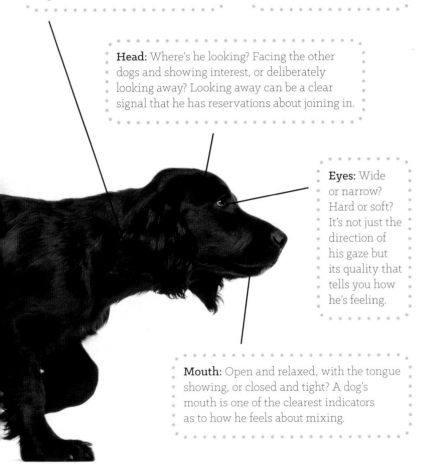

Overall stance: How a dog is standing when he's near other dogs can tell you a lot. Stiff and still? Not usually a good sign. Loose and relaxed? Probably open to some social contact.

Ears: Up or down? Forward or back? Ears are great for spotting a dog's degree of interest or intentness, and easy-to-read ears can also reveal a degree of discomfort.

Head: Where's he looking? Facing the other dogs and showing interest, or deliberately looking away? Looking away can be a clear signal that he has reservations about joining in.

Eyes: Wide or narrow? Hard or soft? It's not just the direction of his gaze but its quality that tells you how he's feeling.

Mouth: Open and relaxed, with the tongue showing, or closed and tight? A dog's mouth is one of the clearest indicators as to how he feels about mixing.

IN THE LOOK

Even behaviorists who dislike anthropomorphic comparisons will usually agree that dogs have particularly expressive eyes. Learn to read the signs: a hard look can be one of the earliest signs of trouble, when a dog isn't feeling comfortable; and soft eyes are the clearest indication of a happy, relaxed dog.

A happy dog's eyes are rounded, though not excessively so, and the muscles around the eye are loose. There isn't any tightness in the dog's face. Sometimes dogs' eyes look slightly "squinty" when relaxed, which is difficult to describe but easy to recognize. At the other end of the mood spectrum is the hard eye that dogs sometimes give one another, a blank, flat look, with the muscles around the eye held tense and tight. This look tends to spell trouble. You might see it when one dog has something another wants, or if a game is about to tip over into something less playful. Unlike humans, dogs don't tend to look one another straight in the eye, and a direct, hard look can therefore be read as confrontational.

LOOK AWAY NOW

It's not strictly a look, but more of a look away, and socially fluent dogs are just as skilled at averting their gaze at tricky moments as they are at expressing themselves with a direct glance. A dog may use a look-away for all sorts of reasons; you might see a shy or nervous dog looking away in "I-can't-even-see-you" mode, when he's at the edge of a situation he's not sure about, and he's avoiding a direct encounter with another dog or dogs. Conversely, a confident dog may use a look-away when he's introducing himself to one that seems less confident. It's a tactic that seems to be used as a deliberately non-confrontational gesture. When you see it combined with a tongue flick (more of that on the following pages), the effect is slightly nervous, while a deliberate look-away combined with a brief, marking-style pee may be used as a signal to reassure and inform others. The dog that offers the latter may, for example, be offering the other dogs the opportunity to come over and sniff out some information about him, while sending a signal that he won't be in their face if they do.

DID YOU KNOW. . .

If a dog's eyes are very wide and exaggeratedly rounded, this tends to indicate a high degree of unwelcome arousal, perhaps stress or fear. The expression may be accentuated by "whale eye," when the sclera, the white of the eye, which isn't usually visible, can be seen as a white rim around the iris.

AROUND THE MOUTH

The mouth tells you just as much as the eyes when you're putting canine expressions together. The corners of the mouth, called the commissure, will show whether a dog is feeling tense or laid back, playful or confrontational. Add in whether his mouth is open or closed and you'll quickly learn to read it.

A relaxed, happy dog will usually have an open mouth with the tongue possibly showing a little. His lips will be loose, without wrinkles. Tight, closed mouths usually indicate a problem at some level; at its most extreme, the commissure will be held tensely and the muzzle around the dog's lips will be in muscular creases. If you looked closely at a very tense dog (and we don't recommend it), you would even see that his whiskers are bristling.

DO DOGS SMILE?

It's a question that vets and behaviorists are used to: my dog seems to grin, but is that really a smile? And the answer is, not in the human sense, no, but that doesn't mean that your dog isn't happy. Some dogs pull back their lips to expose their teeth, while keeping the corners of their mouths relaxed, and the resulting expression, though probably originating in submissive behavior, does look very much like a smile. It's certainly not the baring of teeth that is part of a keep-away display from a dog that feels under threat. It's most often seen when a dog is relaxed, at home, perhaps lolling on the sofa or in his bed. There's even an appealing theory that dogs have learned the "smile" from sustained interactions with people, although unfortunately this hasn't yet been substantiated by science.

TONGUE FLICKS

These are used a lot, by almost every dog, but you may not notice them as a separate piece of communication until you pause to look. A tongue flick looks the way it sounds, a fast flip of the tongue along the side of a dog's mouth or over his nose. One study found that dogs don't tongue flick when there aren't other dogs or people around, so it's reasonable to assume that a dog that does it is sending a deliberate signal. Dogs seem to use them to signal slight discomfort (for example, if they're being petted when they'd prefer to be left alone) or as an appeasing signal (for example, if they have to pass a dog they're doubtful about). Used on their own, they are low-key signs that the user doesn't pose a challenge or threat to others, but would perhaps prefer not to be bothered or hassled.

ALL EARS

The easiest canine ears to read are those that are naturally large, pointed, and upright, such as those of a German shepherd, say, or a husky. The hardest are exaggeratedly long drooping ears, such as those of a bloodhound or even the more moderate "drop" of a pointer.

If you look closely at the muscles at the base of the ear, it's possible to see what's going on with most breeds, although you might have a problem "reading" a few of the heavily "disguised" dogs, such as the extremely long and silky ears of an Afghan hound.

EARS FORWARD

Ears are an important part of the signaling system, helping dogs to express arousal, strong interest, discomfort, stress, aggression, or fear. Very broadly, ears "pricking" or moving forward and upright from the neutral position signify interest, and as they move further forward, the level of focus is growing. Ears pinned back generally signal discomfort or withdrawal. There are any number of degrees of ear position between the extremes of high alert and fearful retreat, but if you look at the way in which a dog is holding its ears and the position of its mouth, you will be able to gauge much more clearly how a dog is feeling.

> ### DID YOU KNOW. . .
> When faced with a fearful dog, not only should you back off and keep your distance, but also turn your body sideways to them. It immediately reduces your perceived threat in dog language.

EARS AND MOUTH

These combinations look at how comfortable, or not, a dog is feeling. The vast majority of bad dog–human encounters come about because someone misread the signals when a dog was extremely uncomfortable or fearful, and persisted in close-up contact when they should have backed off. Fear is by far the most common cause of aggression in dogs.

Ears forward
Slightly: Mild interest
Moderately: Increasing interest
Strongly: High alert

Ears neutral:
Nothing to get excited about

Ears back
Slightly: Disengagement; mild discomfort
Moderately: Discomfort; apprehension
Strongly, pinned back against head:
Very uncomfortable; fearful

Mouth closed
Face relaxed, muscles loose: Neutral
Face tight, wrinkled muzzle:
Uncomfortable; may be moving
to fear-based aggression

Mouth open
Loose lips, perhaps lolling tongue:
Comfortable; relaxed
Lips held back from teeth, wrinkled muzzle:
Uncomfortable; apprehensive

TAIL TALK

The way dogs hold their tails tells other dogs a lot, but it is probably also responsible for some of the greatest misunderstandings between dogs and people. Humans have mostly been told from childhood that a happy dog wags his tail, whereas in fact there are different types and degrees of tail-wag, and they're not always signs of good cheer.

WHAT KIND OF WAG?

Here's what you should look for when a dog wags his tail: is it fast or slow, low or high, sweeping or stiff? If you see, say, a golden retriever (one of the easiest types of tail to read, because it is mobile, long, and furry) holding its tail at mid-height and wagging in a loose, sweeping motion, it's likely that he's cheerful and relaxed. A slow wag with a tail held stiffly and quite high, though, can mean something else altogether: it's usually the sign of an alert dog, who may be uneasy about a situation. Add in any possible sensitivity about place—for example, if the same dog is sending the slow-wag signal while standing in his basket—and it would be unwise for anyone, person or dog, to approach him. Very broadly, a stiff tail wag tends to send a warning, and the slower it is, the stronger the warning. A relaxed tail is held mid-height; a tail held higher means the dog is on high alert; and a lowered, or even a tucked tail indicates discomfort or even fear.

HARD-TO-READ TAILS

Of course, some tails are much easier to read than others. Retrievers, Labradors, and, now that tail-docking is increasingly restricted, and even banned, breeds such as poodles and pointers are all fluent tail communicators. Dogs with naturally abbreviated or curly tails, such as pugs, or those that carry their tails both higher than most and/or in a curl, such as Samoyeds, aren't ever going to tell human observers much through their tails, so you may have to rely on the other signs their bodies send.

LEFT OR RIGHT?

Aside from whether a tail "wag" is stiff or relaxed, there's another factor that's recently been spotted in dog-to-dog tail speak. A research project at the University of Trento in Italy looked at whether dogs respond differently if another dog wags its tail from left to right, or right to left. The results showed that dogs' stress levels became raised if they saw another dog wagging to the left, but they remained relaxed if the dog was wagging to the right. Other dogs were also less hesitant in approaching a right-wagging dog. The project highlights that there is still plenty to discover about how dogs communicate with each other. And it's ongoing; the next question researchers want to answer is whether the "directional" wag is made as a conscious signal to others, or whether it is a piece of unconscious body language.

ADDING IT UP

Usually we know our own dogs very well, and we are so used to interpreting their moods and behaviors when they're interacting with us that we hardly notice we're doing it. Watching different dogs in a lot of different situations helps us to see both their similarities and their differences, and to spot the various ways in which they express themselves, from the tops of their ears to the tips of their tails.

The bonus is that when you are familiar with both the positive and the negative signs in dogs' body language, you can relax through positive encounters, but move in and distract your dog if any discomforts arise before a dog–dog situation becomes really tense. It's also enjoyable when you become fluent enough to pick out the personalities of different dogs. When you're watching a group, it becomes easy to spot the up-for-anything fun-lover, the on-the-periphery shy dog who's a little fearful of joining in, the off-the-scale barker, who sounds loud and pushy but who's just enjoying himself, and the dreaded play policeman, who's determined to manage a play session, even though his attention isn't really needed.

BREAKS AND PAUSES

In between expressive play, with plenty of all-systems-go body language to spot, you'll also notice that dogs introduce plenty of pauses when they are interacting. Short breaks, with the postures that go with them, are also signaled clearly dog-to-dog, and they are often marked by play bows, tongue flicks, and shake-offs.

Play bows often open a game between dogs, acting as an invitation. But they can also mark a few seconds' time out, and in a chase game, a brief pause followed by a play bow seems to serve as notice that the chaser will now become the chasee, or vice versa.

Shake-offs are just as they sound: a dog will give a brief, sharp, all-over shake, usually before turning to do something else. They aren't just used in company with other dogs; a dog may shake off between waking up and deciding on an activity, say, or before focusing on a toy and starting a game with his human companions.

Tongue-flicks can often be seen when a dog is exiting a situation. Some behaviorists have identified them as part of a canine "excuse me," as a dog, for whatever reason, decides to absent himself.

CANINE EQUATIONS

Use what you've learned about dogs' body language to try out some deductions about what a dog may be feeling, taking into account the situation he's in. Just as you would with a person, you have to add up the various signals sent by their facial expressions and their body language to get a reasonably accurate idea of what they're "saying." If you're with dogs mixing freely together, it can also tell you if all is well, or if a game may be at a tip-over point, with the dogs becoming overexcited, to the point where it will lead to conflict.

Here is a handful of examples of whole-body language you may see when dogs are together.

Looking away + relaxed, sweeping tail and body line + loose open mouth, tongue showing = He's happy enough. But the look away may tell you that he's either taking a little time out or he's using reassuring body language directed toward another, less-relaxed dog.

In play, with tight mouth + hard, focused eyes + upright tail, wagging stiffly = He's showing signs that the game may be becoming too intense. You could call him out, or offer a group distraction (such as a treat giveaway) to let the body language loosen up a bit.

On his own, with low body line + looking away, eyes averted + tail tucked = He's looking like a fearful dog. Whatever is worrying him, he doesn't want to be there. You, or if he's not yours, his owner, should take him out of the situation that is making him uncomfortable.

Moving in on a playing group, with ears tight forward + mouth closed = A distraction is called for here. You may be looking at a "play policeman" who has decided it's his business to manage the game.

Playing chase with another dog, low body line + tail held stiffly + head lowered + tight commissure, mouth closed = signs that play is moving into prey drive. Call the dogs and distract them.

CHAPTER 9: HOW TUNED IN IS YOUR DOG?

Most owners play with their dogs, whether they opt for simple games of fetch in the backyard or more structured hide-and-seek or agility exercises. This chapter offers you a mix of games and tests that will help to give you an idea of how tuned in your dog is to you, and how clever and quick to learn he is in certain areas. They may stretch his thinking a little, too. Remember, they're supposed to be fun for both parties (and there aren't any "right" or "wrong" outcomes), so if your dog isn't showing interest in a particular activity, drop it and move on. There's something here for most abilities, especially if his involvement is reinforced by rewards of favorite treats or a quick game in between exercises.

STARTING OUT

With the number of available canine cognition studies increasing, people have become more and more interested in testing their dogs' abilities. If you're used to playing the same old favorites together, trying something different from the options on the following pages may prompt you to observe your dog closely again, and refresh your knowledge of his actions and reactions in different situations. Whether or not he "wins" at the activities, make sure he gets plenty of praise just for taking part; the more enthusiasm you show, the more likely it is to be reflected in your pet.

DID YOU KNOW. . .
Although dogs are far less closely related to humans than members of the great ape family are, thousands of years of living very closely together have given them a closer understanding of human body language, gestures, and intelligence than our nearest genetic relatives, chimpanzees.

DO DOGS FEEL PLEASED WITH THEMSELVES?

You'll know that sense of achievement you have when you've worked hard to learn something or to solve a problem and you manage it, but does your dog have the same feeling when he successfully learns something new? A recent Swedish study that tested dogs on six different tasks, some quite difficult, indicated that dogs may experience a pleasurable "eureka moment" when they solve something, just as people do. Dogs given rewards at random didn't respond with the same level of excitement and pleasure as those who worked to reach a positive result and were then given a reward, even if the tester didn't reinforce their achievement with lots of praise. Look out for the signs of excitement that show that your dog knows just how clever he's been.

MIX IT UP

Don't always try the same exercises in the same order and in the same place; instead, move them around. Give your dog a quick refresher on a walk in the park, or add in an exercise in the middle of a game (or even a grooming session). In other words, stay flexible and try out new ideas as they come to you. You'll find that your pet appreciates you all the more when you keep things fresh and sometimes surprise him with the unexpected.

THINGS TO REMEMBER

When you're working on something new, it pays to bear the following pointers in mind:

- If your dog doesn't show any interest in an activity when you've offered it a few times, don't keep pushing it. Move on; you can revisit it and try again later.

- Make sure the food rewards you offer are small but high-value, something your dog really loves. Cheese or small pieces of chicken often hit the spot.

- Keep it short and fun. A daily focused game-or-test session of around ten minutes is plenty, and it will maintain your dog's enthusiasm better than a really long session once a week.

ONE, TWO, THREE, YAWN

When one person yawns, particularly in slightly soporific circumstances—say, the last hour of the working day in a stuffy room—it's usual that a number of other people will follow suit. Yawning can be contagious. But what about with dogs—if you yawn, will your pet start to yawn, too? Here's how to test your dog's bonding in the simplest possible way.

Try this at a quiet time of day when your dog isn't racing around. You'll need a chair and a timer.

1. Sit down near your dog and start to yawn. Make the most of it, with plenty of noise.

2. Yawn every ten seconds, for a minute. Keep an eye on your dog.

60 secs

3. At the end of the minute, set the timer for a two-minute alert. Watch your dog to see if he yawns before the timer sounds.

x2

HOW DID HE DO?

- If he yawned within the first minute, while you were still yawning, he's exhibiting an unusually high degree of empathy.

- If he yawned within the subsequent two minutes, after you'd stopped yawning, he has a strong bond with you.

- If he didn't yawn at all, he's a more independent type. This doesn't mean that the two of you aren't close, just that he doesn't observe you as closely as he might.

DID YOU KNOW...

Never underestimate how closely your dog watches you for visual signs of what you are doing or thinking. The "sixth sense" often attributed to dogs is thought by some behaviorists to be explained by the fact that our dogs watch us considerably more than we watch them, and they use their close and constant observation to work out what our next actions will be.

NOW YOU SEE IT...

Does your dog always want to please you? Or does he play along any time he's being observed by you, doing whatever works to his own advantage when you're not watching him? This game looks at whether your pet is willing to take a treat, even if you've asked him not to, and at whether or not watching him do it makes a difference.

You'll need a helper, a timer, and a few high-value treats.

• •

1. Ask your helper to stand next to your dog, holding him on a loose leash, and ask him to sit. Stand facing them about 10 feet (3m) away.

2. Put a treat on the floor in the middle of the space between you. Look at your dog and say "no" firmly (if he is used to "leave" or any other equivalent command, use the word he's familiar with).

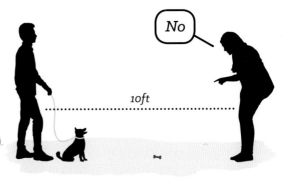

No

10ft

3. Ask your helper to let the leash go, and start the timer.

Start

4. Cover your eyes with your hands (you can look between your fingers to watch what's happening).

5. As soon as your dog moves forward and eats the treat, your helper should stop the timer.

Stop

6. If your dog hasn't taken the treat after a timed half-minute, take your hands away from your face and give him the treat.

Repeat the game three or four times to see if your dog consistently takes the treat, or waits for your "permission"—or a mix of the two.

HOW DID HE DO?

- If he took the treat shortly after you covered your face, it's an indication that he'll operate independently, if he isn't observed.

- If he waited until you "released" him and gave him the treat, he tends to work with you and wait on your direction (you'll find that even half a minute is quite a long wait, if you are all three standing in silence).

MORE OR LESS?

Does your dog know about relative quantities? And can he decide to pick the smaller quantity from two sets of treats, so long as he's rewarded for doing so? You can find out with this test. You need a big handful of very small treats to practice with. The idea is to get him to pick between different quantities—at first, quantities with a very pronounced difference, then, as he gets used to the idea, an ever-smaller one.

1. Pick up ten treats in one hand, and three in the other (take them from a bowl on a raised surface, so that your dog can't see what you're doing). Close your hands around them.

2. Ask your dog to sit, and kneel down facing him about 3 feet (1m) away. Hold out your closed hands with the treats inside, then turn your hands palm side up and open them.

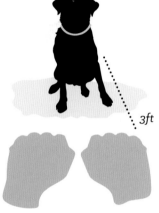

3ft

Uh-uh

3. Let your dog approach, and say "less." If he goes to the hand with fewer treats, let him eat them, repeating "less" as he does so. If he goes for the hand with more treats, say, "Uh-uh," close your hands, ask him to sit, and begin again.

4. When he chooses the "less" hand, allow him to eat both those treats and, afterward, the ones from the "more" hand.

Try not to talk too much; simply say either "less" or "uh-uh," and give him time to think and react, so he can focus on working out the clue, without any other distractions.

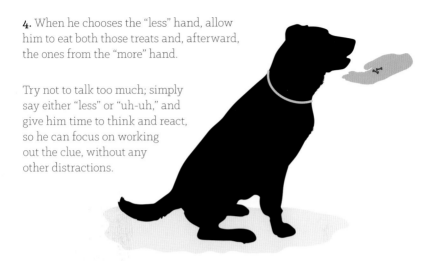

Most dogs will understand within a few repetitions that if they choose the lesser number of treats, they'll get to eat all the treats, and if they go for the larger number, they won't get any. Change the hand that is holding the smaller number of treats around, so that the choice for your dog is more complex than simply choosing the left or right hand.

HOW DID HE DO?

- If he learned "less" within eight or ten repetitions, try reducing the difference between the number of treats—for example, from ten and three to eight and five, and then to six and four. The smaller the difference, the harder it becomes for him to make the right pick.

- If he's clearly finding it hard to pick the "less" hand, make it a little easier for him by keeping the "more" hand closed for just a little longer, to nudge him toward the right choice.

- If your dog can learn the game well enough to pick "less" when the treat balance is down to six and four, he's extremely smart. But you'd better stop the game now, before he bursts!

THE SHELL GAME

The shell game is a version of the old cup and ball game, in which a ball is hidden under one of several cups, which are then moved around speedily, and you have to guess which cup conceals the ball. This is the doggy version. Basically, treats are hidden under upside-down cups, and your dog has to find them. It's not complicated, but you start by confusing the dog's nose, so less-visually sharp dogs may find it more challenging. And if your dog turns out to be a champion at it, you can easily ramp up the difficulty to make him work a little harder.

You need three opaque plastic cups (light enough for your dog to turn over) and a handful of small, high-value treats. Rub a treat all over the cups, inside and out, before you start—this makes it harder for him to find the treat by scent alone.

Be patient when showing your dog this exercise, and make sure he has understood each step and is locating the treat in each case, before moving on to the next step.

- -

1. With your dog watching, hide a treat under a cup. Encourage him to come and turn the cup over to get the treat. Do this a few times, until he understands the action of turning over the cup to reach the reward.

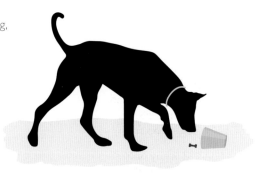

2. Line the cups up in a row, and let your dog watch you place a treat under one of them. Encourage him to come over to them, but don't let him turn them over; instead, wait until he noses the one with the treat, then turn it over yourself and give him the treat. Repeat this several times, putting the treat under different cups in the row. After a few rounds, he will probably be nosing the right cup.

3. When he's getting the right cup and receiving the treat on most attempts, move the cups around after you put the treat under the cup, and before he's encouraged to come and find it. Even if dogs watch the "switch around" sequence, they often find it hard to then correctly locate the treat. Give him plenty of praise (as well as the treat) when he gets it right.

HOW DID HE DO?

• If he was enthusiastic about step 1 and managed step 2, but continued, even after lots of tries, to pick the wrong cups, he may not be a master of deduction. Keep trying step 2, but hold off on step 3 for a while.

• If he moved easily onto step 3, but then could only find the treat if the cups were moved just one space over, and you did it slowly and deliberately, he's good, but not yet five-star rated.

• If he got to step 3 and is managing to find the treat, even after you've moved the cups speedily and swapped them around several times, he's a shell-game natural. See how complex you can make the cup-moving—this dog won't get frustrated if you ramp up the difficulty.

POINT, YOU PICK

Canine cognition experts attach a lot of importance to whether or not a dog seems to understand, or to act on, a pointing gesture made by a person. In general, animals don't "read" gestures made by other species, much less use them to make a decision on how they themselves are going to behave. So it's significant if your dog seems to understand when you point; it indicates that he's working with you and that may make him a natural for teamwork.

You'll need a helper for this game, and a handful of high-value treats for your dog (he'll be eating quite a lot of them, so keep them small).

- -

1. Ask your friend to hold your dog, and stand about 10 feet (3m) apart, without any obstacles between you.

2. Place two treats on the ground in front of you, one to each side. Standing between them, point to one of the treats.

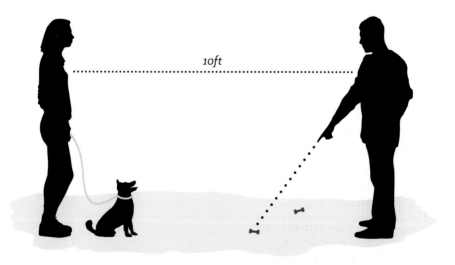

10ft

3. While you're still pointing, your friend should let your dog go. If he's been trained to a release command, such as "OK," they can use that, too, as they release him.

OK

x 10

4. Your dog will go to the treats. Take a note of which treat he takes first, the one you're pointing to, or the other one. He should be free to eat both treats; you're just noting which he goes for first.

Repeat the exercise ten times, keeping note of which treat your dog goes to first each time. After the tenth repeat, score your dog.

HOW DID HE DO?

- If he went to the treat you were pointing at most of the time, your dog is keen to work with you, and happy to take a collaborative approach to "problem solving" (i.e., which treat to eat first).

- If his tendency was to go to the treat you weren't pointing at, you may have a more independent thinker, and one who is naturally more self-reliant.

- And what if his selection appeared to be random? Your dog may simply not have learned what it means when you point (not all do), or he may attach no particular importance to it.

HOT OR COLD?

This is an exercise that calls for consistency, patience, and a strong connection with your dog. The idea behind it is to encourage dogs to think for themselves and to try things out, until they gradually deduce what you're asking them to do—that is, you're "shaping" their behavior. It's a standard activity in the behavior-shaping repertoires of many trainers. Use your tone of voice to give "hot" and "cold" meaning—they don't have inherent meaning for him; he's learning what they infer.

To start, you decide what it is you'd like your dog to do. Maybe his favorite stuffed toy is lying in the middle of the floor and you'd like him to walk over to it and pick it up. You're not going to ask him to do that, though. You're simply going to cue him with the words "hot" and "cold," and use treats to reinforce "hot," when he's getting closer to what you want him to do.

Start with a toy in the middle of the room, with your dog present, and a stash of treats. It's best for you to direct things sitting down, as you don't want to give him body-language cues, just voice ones. Use a controlled but upbeat tone for the "hot" cue and a lower, neutral tone for the "cold" cue.

· ·

1. Watch your dog carefully. When he moves in the direction of the toy, even if it's just a step or two, say "hot" and throw him a treat.

Hot

Cold

2. If he then moves away from the toy, say "cold" in a quiet voice. No treat. If he moves back in the direction of the toy (or further toward it), say "hot," and treat again.

3. Carry on with this, engaging with him and carefully watching exactly which way he's moving, keeping up the "hot" and "cold" cues. Smart dogs often catch on to this surprisingly quickly and start trying out which behavior is going to win them more treats. You can use "hot" in a more excited tone the nearer he gets to "solving" the puzzle.

Hot!

4 When he reaches the ultimate "hot"—in this case, locating and picking up the toy—use the "hot" cue excitedly and give him a treat bonus.

If your dog comes directly to you and tries to mug you for more treats, fold your arms and completely ignore him. He'll quickly understand that this isn't how he'll earn them.

HOW DID HE DO?

- If he was looking around and then at you, and evidently thinking things over with an eye to more treats, even if he didn't easily reach the goal you had in mind, try repeating the exercise. He'll probably get it eventually, and then you can start varying the goals.

- If he clearly found it baffling (and some dogs do), try again another day, but don't push it if he's clearly becoming frustrated at not understanding what you want. This is harder for some dogs than others.

FIND YOUR TOY

This isn't a new game, but it's one that encourages dogs both to play "find" and to distinguish between different things and to make deduction-based choices. Many dogs can learn to "name" a wide variety of objects; others seem to struggle with the difference between an action and an object, and find it hard to distinguish between toys. You'll probably discover which category your pet fits into quite quickly—if it turns out he's a natural name-checker, great. It's an activity you can both enjoy indefinitely.

However, if he has problems with distinguishing between just one or two items by name, this may not be his game. Try two or three times and, if he still isn't managing it, don't persist; some studies have shown that this tends to be a "can or can't" exercise, and you don't want him to become frustrated to the point where it inhibits him from playing and interacting with you.

To play the game, you need a number of toys that your dog is used to playing with. There's no time limit—if your dog enjoys learning the names for different things, you can make it a daily practice—so take your time. You should be sure that he really does know the name of one object before you try to add another. You may find that he already knows the names of some of his most familiar toys because you use them with him more regularly than you realize.

· ·

1. Take your dog's favorite toy and play a game with him, focusing on and naming the toy and stressing the name as you do so. If, for example, it's a stuffed bear, say "take your bear," and repeat the name as you play.

Take your bear!

2. Repeat the exercise in short sessions until your dog begins to recognize the toy by name.

Find your bear!

3. Take the bear and "hide" it, somewhere easy to find, while your dog is watching—perhaps behind a chair. Add "find" to your communication: "Find your bear!" If your dog doesn't immediately catch on, run and find the bear with him. Again, repeat until he's comfortable finding the toy.

4. When he's regularly finding one named toy, play the same game with another. So the stages are the same, but "your bear" might become "your ball."

Take your ball!

Find your bear!

5. When he seems familiar with both named toys, lay them side by side on the floor, approach them with your dog, and ask him to "find" a specific one. If he picks it up first time, give him lots of praise. If he picks up the other toy, say, "Uh-uh," take it, and lay it back down, then ask him to "find the…" again.

6. When he's regularly finding the toy you've singled out from the two choices, add a third, and take him through the steps again. In between regular sessions encouraging him to pick one toy out, play with all of them individually, ensuring you use their names.

7. When he's making the correct choice from a lineup of three toys, you're set to build his vocabulary, adding to the number as he learns the new names.

Find your bone!

HOW DID HE DO?

- If he can learn to identify three or more toys over a period of time, he's a natural, and you'll be able to add more.

- If he learned the first one easily, but then seemed to stall, take your time with the second toy, and play with both separately for a while to reinforce their names, before putting them together and asking him to pick.

- If he seems frustrated and bewildered about what it is you want him to do after two or three short learning sessions, try another game. Research has shown that this game isn't for every dog.

SNEAKY DOG

Based on the idea behind a project at the University of Zurich, this is by far the most complicated exercise you're going to try with your dog, but it's fascinating to see whether he'll work out that he needs to be sneaky in order to get the maximum possible number of treats.

Marianne Heberlein, the dog cognition expert behind the original study, had watched two pet dogs deceive one another to get something they both wanted. For example, one dog might run to the window and pretend to look at something interesting, then, when the second dog came to see what was going on, would rush to occupy the prime sunny spot that the second dog had left. Heberlein wondered if dogs would behave in the same way with humans, if given the opportunity, and set up an exercise to test it out.

Sneaky Dog is a simplified version of the original research, but it still takes a little effort to set up, and needs several consecutive days to reach a result, so maybe it is one to try out as a holiday project, when you have plenty of time. You'll need two helpers (you can't be one of them, as you have a separate part to play in the final stage of the experiment, and ideally you shouldn't be present on days one to four, when your "good" and "bad" humans are interacting with your dog), plus a selection of high-value treats and duller treats (such as plain dog biscuits).

DAYS 1 & 2

Ask your two helpers to interact with your dog several times a day. On different occasions, person one shows him a high-value treat, then gives it to him; person two shows him a high-value treat and then puts it away in their pocket.

Person 1

Person 2

DAYS 3 & 4

The two same people repeatedly, but on separate occasions, lead your dog
to a box with a treat inside that he can see. Again, person one opens the
box and gives him the treat, while person two opens the box and puts the
treat in their pocket. By the end of day 4, most dogs will have developed a
perception of person one as the good guy, and person two as the frustrating,
bad guy—or the "competitive partner" in research terminology.

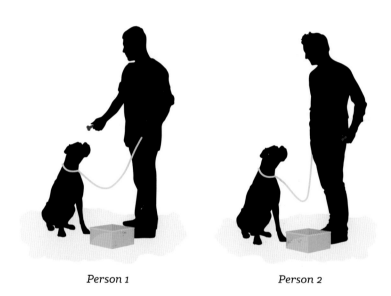

Person 1   *Person 2*

DAYS 5 & 6

1. Set up three boxes
with transparent lids.
One has a high-value
treat inside; one has a
relatively dull biscuit;
and the third is empty.

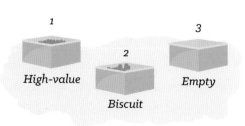

2. Your dog should be led to the boxes on various occasions through the day by person one and person two, and the first box he sniffs at is opened. As he becomes used to the routine, he'll start to lead the way to the boxes, as this may result in a treat being given. As usual, person one gives him whatever is inside, while person two puts the treat or biscuit in their pocket. If he picks the empty box, he doesn't get a treat.

Person 1

3. After each test, you return to the room, and the other people leave it. Walk over to the boxes with your dog and pick up the one he goes to first. If there's a treat in it, he can eat it, but if it's empty, you just show him the box.

Repeat the process ten or twelve times, and keep a record of which box your dog went to on each occasion.

Person 2

HOW DID HE DO?

In Heberlein's experiment, the dogs seemed to have worked out that if they took person two to a box containing a treat, they never got to eat it, whereas if they took person one to the same box, they'd get the treat. They also knew that when they took their owner to a box, if it still contained a treat, they'd be given it.

The results showed that a number of dogs had learned to act on their knowledge—they took "mean" person two to the empty box more often (since it didn't have a treat, they weren't using up their chances of getting both treats), and person one to the high-value treat more often. Once they'd had the high-value treat, they would use stage two of the exercise to take their owners to the duller treat, in the knowledge that they would get that, too.

- Count the times on days 5 and 6 that your dog led person two to the empty box, and person one to the high-value treat. Add in the times in the second stage of the exercise that he led you to the remaining box that contained a treat.

- If, across days 5 and 6, he gradually increases the number of times that he takes person two to the empty box, and the number of times he takes person one and you, his owner, to the boxes that contain treats, you have a savvy dog who has learned from experience that being a little sneaky can work for him.

Not every dog will manage to work this exercise out to his best advantage, but if your dog does, he definitely has above-average deductive (or manipulative!) skills.

WORKING WITH RELUCTANT DOGS

What if your pet isn't keen to engage on different activities with you? Not all dogs take easily to new or more complicated games or exercises. This may be for a variety of reasons, so here are some ideas to get him out of his rut.

It's certainly not true that you can't teach an old dog new tricks, but an older dog may not always feel he can be bothered with anything complex, unless there are some very desirable rewards on offer.

Here are a few things you can try, to motivate a reluctant dog:

- Keep sessions to five minutes or less—don't pick the longer options. Although this sounds very brief, you'll find that it's longer than it sounds when he's concentrating.

- Reward smaller steps, and if he's having trouble with something, see if you can help. For example, in the shell game, you can tap the right cup and see if he follows your clue.

- Don't try playing anything complicated when he's already tired. If you've just taken a long walk, it's probably not the moment to introduce something new.

- Mix up the familiar and the new, with an emphasis on the familiar. For example, if your older dog loves a game of fetch, play fetch with him for a little while, then try five minutes of the first and simplest steps of "Find Your Toy," and finish up with another short fetch session.

- Finish even a short play or exercise session with something you know he can do—even if it's just a simple "sit"—and reward him for doing it. Ending interactions on a positive note will make him more enthusiastic for next time.

IF YOU CAN'T SEEM TO GET YOUR DOG TO CONCENTRATE

Maybe you have the opposite problem—rather than lacking enthusiasm, you've got a dog who is so energetic that he can't seem to think or focus. If getting him to calm down enough to think about the problem at hand seems impossible, think about trying some different tactics:

- Take him for a long, active walk before you try anything more cerebral. If he's already tired, he may find it easier to settle down to some mental exercise.

- Alternate more active and "thinking" exercises, and try playing a game he likes, and in which he interacts with you, like tug, in gaps between them.

- Make sure he has the "sit" cue well mastered, so that you can get him to pause if he starts getting over-excited.

- Use a low voice and calm body language, except when you actually want him to act excited. A low-pitched tone can help to calm excitable dogs.

CHAPTER 10: BUILDING THE BOND

Now you know more about your dog's world view, it's time to find some new ways to spend downtime together. Whether you opt for laying a treat trail, learning canine massage, or simply dreaming up some different activities you can share, you'll find that with a little imagination owners as well as dogs can learn new tricks.

LAYING A TREAT TRAIL

You've probably already played a find-the-treat game with your dog. This is a slightly more complex version in which you gradually reduce the clues (size and overt smelliness of treats) that you're giving your dog, encouraging him to work his nose a little harder to reap the reward. Some dog classes practice "nosework," offering dogs the chance to give their noses a good workout by locating the source of a smell (sometimes very faint, and from a well-concealed source), and this is the at-home version.

Allow your dog around fifteen minutes per treat-hunting session. He may not need it at first, but as you cut back on the strength of the smells he's tracking, he's likely to need more time.

Try not to indicate the hiding places to your dog; owners find it hard not to "cue" their dogs by glancing at where a treat is hidden, or angling their bodies toward it, and all dogs are virtuosos when it comes to picking up human body language. If you can't help yourself, you can make the hunt more challenging for both you and your dog by asking someone else to hide the treats before you come into the room. Use high-value treats, such as pea-sized pieces of cheese or chicken.

Leaving your dog outside the room, hide ten treats. Vary the height and difficulty of access, but keep them relatively easy for a first try. Let your dog into the room, then show him the first treat, and the second if necessary. After that, leave him to himself to find the rest, keeping track and stopping only when he's found them all. If you're worried about unintentional cuing, sit down and don't watch him as he hunts. If he stops before he's found them all, encourage him to keep going in an enthusiastic voice, but after the first two, don't lead him.

On subsequent days, repeat the exercise in exactly the same way, but each time cut down the size of the treats slightly and increase the difficulty of the hiding places.

Eventually, your dog should be able to track down ten tiny treats wrapped in twists of paper and very well hidden. By gradually building the challenge of the exercise, you're encouraging him to rely on his nose more and more as he tracks them down.

DID YOU KNOW. . .

All dogs have exceptional scenting skills, but some recent research has shown that pet dogs, living in a human, sight-biased world, are coming to rely less on their sense of smell. Playing scent-based games with your dog will help him to keep his number-one sense well honed.

BACKYARD WORKOUT: SETTING UP AGILITY GAMES AT HOME

Most people don't have the space (or the inclination) to install a full set of agility equipment in their yard, but there are plenty of agility games you can play with your dog, using inexpensive or improvised equipment. If your dog turns out to love going through his agility moves with you, consider enrolling him in a local agility class with a complete set of kit, where he can be put through his paces with a group of other enthusiastic dogs.

Tackle each of these four exercises individually, encouraging your dog to:

- weave through a line of cones or poles;
- run through a light nylon-fabric play tunnel;
- pause for a count of three at a set spot (sitting or standing)—the equivalent of the pause table on a real agility course;
- clear several jumps of an appropriate height.

Apart from the play tunnel and something to "mark" the pause point (a small mat, for example), you'll need a set of twelve inexpensive plastic cones (these are like traffic cones but smaller and lighter). The ones sold for agility have holes in the sides, so that you can feed a pole through them and use them as jump supports.

Some dogs are naturals at agility exercises; they watch once or twice, are lured through the trickier parts with treats, and then perform flawlessly. Others need plenty of excited, upbeat verbal encouragement and quite a few treats, as well as many more repetitions. Most enjoy the fact that you're jogging alongside them as they work even the simplest course.

SAFETY FIRST

If you improvise, be careful that any equipment is set up safely. Don't use heavy pieces, such as ladders, to stand in for jumps, for example. And be sure that your dog is physically fit enough for the games. Generally, jumps shouldn't be higher than the shoulder height of the dog. Finally, if you have a very young or a very old dog, or if your pet has suffered from back problems, avoid jumping altogether.

DID YOU KNOW. . .

Tiny dogs can be just as good at agility tasks as larger ones. Tic Tac, tipping the scales at just 2lb 8oz (1.1kg), and hailing from Milwaukee, Wisconsin, is thought to be the world's smallest agility dog. The challenge facing the littlest canine competitors is packing enough weight to tip the teeter-totter, or seesaw, element of the course.

WEAVING

Set up four plastic cones in a straight row, leaving even gaps between them, wide enough for your dog to walk through. Your dog should start to weave, leading with his left shoulder (as they do in agility classes), with the second cone to his right. Hold a treat just above and in front of his nose and lure him through the cones. If you have to give him the treat halfway, take out another and continue luring.

After a couple of tries, cut down to a single treat, which should be given to him as he completes the "course." Eventually, you should be able to cut out the treat altogether and simply encourage him through, running alongside him as he weaves. When he reaches this stage, you can add cones to make a longer row, and move them slightly closer together so that he gets used to moving his body in a tighter "weave." In a true agility course, the cones will be replaced by rows of either six or twelve weave poles, but the moves are the same.

TUNNEL

On an agility course, dogs need to run through the tunnel, despite the fact that they may not be able to see the opening at the other end. When your dog is trying the tunnel out for the first time, lay it straight, so that he can see where he's going, and encourage him through. If he's reluctant, lay a treat a little way inside one end of the tunnel, then, as he enters, run to the other end and be ready with another treat as he exits. Lay the tunnel on a curve only when he's running through it happily and without pausing.

PAUSE MAT

On a real agility course, the pause table is the place where highly excited dogs have to wait and collect themselves for a few seconds, even when they're raring to go. Your pause mat serves the same purpose, although in the backyard version, your dog is unlikely to have built up too much steam by the time he reaches it. Ask him to sit, then use a long, low "waaaait" cue to slow him down, and count to five aloud, building the suspense before encouraging him to take off again.

JUMPS

Make these with cones and plastic poles. They're light enough not to hurt your dog, if he misjudges and knocks into them. Many dogs will happily jump to their shoulder height first go, but if you have a less confident jumper, set the pole as low as it will go for the first few attempts, so that your dog can simply hop an inch or two over it. Run alongside him as he approaches, and use a treat to lure him over, if necessary.

When your dog has practiced all four exercises, put the elements together in a very simple course, leaving as much space as possible between them, and making sure there's enough room for your pet to take off and land. The "course" will take only a couple of minutes to set up and take down, and you can practice as often as he, or you, likes.

DOWNTIME BONDING: TEN MINUTES PER DAY

Most dogs like the security of routine, and our pets are such familiar presences in our lives that we tend to fall into regular patterns with them, playing the same games, going on the same walks, and even feeding them the same food. But a recent study on aging in dogs found that those pets that faced some level of challenge in their day-to-day lives tended to be more alert and engaged with what was going on around them, and also remained more lively and active as they aged. Just like us, dogs need variety in their lives as well as routine.

THE 10-MINUTE RULE

Ten minutes doesn't sound like very long, but setting a short time window for new activities means that introducing them is achievable for you every day, even when you're busy. And it's a small investment, if it helps your pet keep his youthful attitude into old age. What should you offer? Variety is key here—try for different activities across a typical week, from teaching a new trick or hunt-the-treat, to buried treasure or an agility challenge. Use your imagination; the idea is to keep switching ideas. Even if you hit on an activity your dog adores, don't do it every day; incorporate it into his regular exercise or playtime and keep introducing new things in his ten-minute time.

On the following pages are some ideas to get you started. Remember, the point is to interact with your dog; it doesn't matter whether a trick or game "works," only that he's intrigued or engaged by a new activity.

DID YOU KNOW. . .

Don't forget that praise can be as effective a reward as a treat for many dogs. Owners whose dogs are treat-motivated sometimes forget the praise part of the equation, but it's good to mix up "rewards," sometimes offering a treat when you get a requested behavior, and sometimes, instead, using a drawn out "goooood dog." Even independent-minded dogs enjoy praise, and research has found that keeping things unpredictable tends to "sharpen" a dog's approach.

TEN-MINUTE EXERCISE

- Take a jog around the block together (make it a time when your dog wouldn't normally be going out—surprise him). No dog minds an extra outing, and many enjoy picking up from a head-down-and-sniff pace.

- If you don't know yet whether or not your dog loves a Frisbee, take him in the yard and try it out. Throw gently at first (and if he turns out to love it, a lighter-weight model especially for dogs will ensure he's never hit too hard by an over-enthusiastic throw).

- Have your dog chase you. You can do this in the yard or in any open space where he's off leash. You can cue him with an excited tone of voice, saying, "Ready? 1, 2, 3…," then simply run away from him. Most dogs love to "catch" their owners and, unlike you chasing him (never a good idea), having him chase you encourages good recall.

- If you have a click-and-release lead, you can make a chase toy that moves by attaching one of his favorite toys to the clip, then alternately extending and releasing the lead catch. This makes the toy "run," which often appeals to dogs with a strong chase instinct. You'll have to be prepared to run yourself to keep him interested.

- Buy a child's canister of bubble mix with a wand and blow bubbles for him; many dogs enjoy trying to catch them.

10-MINUTE TRICK TRAINING

- If you have a hula-hoop on hand, see if your dog will jump through it. Start by holding it just an inch or two from the ground and luring him through with a treat, then gradually raise the height if he likes the idea.

- Try to teach your dog something simple, using the "do as I do" method (see page 116). This could be as straightforward as walking around an obstacle; keep it easy, and see how he does.

- If your dog knows a "leave" command and an "OK" release cue, try it out in different situations. Build toward placing a treat on his paw and having him wait a few seconds before eating it. Start with a two-second leave (it's longer than it sounds), and build the time to five seconds.

10-MINUTE FOOD GAMES

- If your dog eats kibble, try scatter-feeding in the yard, using part of your dog's regular meal and throwing it on the grass. Many dogs enjoy nosing out a handful of biscuits and vacuuming them up, piece by piece, and even the most elderly or arthritic dog can manage it.

- Run a string through a Kong or other food-stuffed toy and hang it from a washing line or other high point. Don't make it too high; the idea is to have your dog work a little harder at extracting the treats, not to strain his back.

- Wrap a few treats in newspaper, then fill an empty cardboard tube with them, and let your dog snuffle them out.

- Try the tennis-ball and muffin tin classic: lay treats into the hollows of a muffin baking tray and put tennis balls over them. Your dog will have to take out a tennis ball to get the treat.

DOWNTIME BONDING: MASSAGE FOR DOGS

The idea of massage for dogs is not a new one; over the last twenty years, classes teaching owners how to massage their pets have become relatively commonplace. You may be doubtful about whether or not massage is really any different from petting a dog, but devotees claim that a massage session relaxes their pet and can help soothe aches and pains, particularly benefiting older dogs.

MASSAGE BASICS

The real test is whether or not your dog enjoys it. Try out some of the strokes described opposite, going slowly and gently, and see if your dog finds them relaxing. If you have to peel him off the floor at the end of a ten-minute session, you can make it a regular treat. If he's unhappy at any part of his body being handled (for example, many dogs don't like their paws being touched), leave it and try another spot.

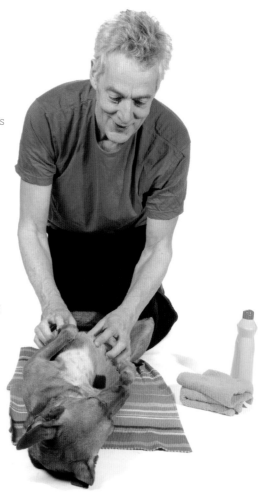

THE THREE KEY STROKES

Compression: A gentle squeezing movement, using both hands

Effleurage: Long, smooth, sweeping strokes, using the whole palm of your hand, and with one hand closely following another

Petrissage: A light, kneading movement using soft pressure from the bottom "V" of the palm (the fingers aren't used)

HOW TO START

Begin when your dog is already pleasantly tired, at a time when he's usually settling down anyway. Early evening is often a good time. You can give your dog a massage on any surface, but it's best to work with him slightly raised from the floor to avoid stressing your own back. A lowish couch or sofa on which he can lie flat works well; a low upholstered stool you can walk all the way around is even better, but use whatever you have. Your dog won't mind if you don't reach every muscle.

Encourage your dog first to sit and then to lie down in position. Lure him with a treat, if you need to. Start by stroking him in a way you know he likes—along his back or down his shoulder, perhaps—using long, slow strokes. As he begins to relax, use compression strokes around his shoulders and neck, working backward along his body. Keep the pressure gentle. Follow up with effleurage, covering the whole length of the body in smooth, even strokes. If he's looking and feeling fully relaxed, use petrissage on his sides and upper legs, and around the back of his neck. Remember to use the lower part of your palm only to make a gentle, rolling, kneading movement. Don't use your fingers. Round the massage off with more effleurage, keeping all your movements slow. If he seems unhappy about having any specific part of his body handled, immediately move on to an area he's happier with.

DOWNTIME BONDING: AROMATHERAPY FOR DOGS

It's one of the more controversial treatments you can offer your dog, but aromatherapy for pets has been increasingly in demand over the last decade. Not everyone believes in its effects, although there are plenty of adherents who swear by it as a relaxation aid for dogs. Aromatherapists who work with animals will also use it to target specific health problems in dogs, ranging from arthritis to anxiety.

HOW DOES IT WORK?

With dogs' super-sensitive smell receptors, it's important to play safe when it comes to using any kind of essential oil. Some people question why dogs would benefit from the kinds of smells that work for humans, given what they often opt to smell when out and about. Aromatherapists treating dogs use more heavily diluted oils than those used for people, but the broad principles are the same: specific smells are used in an animal or person's environment, and sometimes applied directly to the body, to relax, stimulate, or otherwise affect their mood and health.

If you'd be interested in trying aromatherapy with your dog, here are a few things it might be useful to consider:

- Don't launch into it without consulting a professional; essential oils can be as powerful as drugstore medication. Do your homework: read up, take a class, visit a pet specialist in aromatherapy, and see how your dog reacts to a session with an expert practitioner before trying anything at home.

- Aromatherapists agree that the quality of the essential oils is key in treatment. Take advice on the very best quality, and remember that good aromatherapy oils will not be cheap.

- Aromatherapists dilute oils when working with dogs, even if they're intended for inhalation at a distance. Oils are used at stronger concentrations for human aromatherapy, so be sure to follow professional advice, not just about which oils to use but also at what strength. And however strongly diluted, oils should never be applied directly to a dog's skin, except by a professional, or put anywhere near his food.

SELF-TREATMENT WITH SCENT: ZOOPHARMACOGNOSY

Applied zoopharmacognosy is a relatively new treatment, whereby animals are encouraged to choose beneficial scents for themselves. It arose from studying ways in which animals in the wild are believed to treat themselves, choosing plants with natural benefits to self-medicate. It's an interesting idea: instead of a therapist choosing essential oils according to which they think will benefit the dog, he is presented with a wide range of oils in bottles and encouraged to choose for himself. The therapist observes the dog's body language and "reads" his interest in specific scents. It has both fans and detractors, and the jury is still out on its scientific standing, but the treatment is attracting a growing number of followers.

THE SMELL OF HOME

One thing that anyone with a pet should do, whether or not they're interested in aromatherapy, is to eliminate existing "scent blasters" from their home. Aromatherapists agree that highly scented synthetic room diffusers and fresheners are likely to be an irritant to dogs' sensitive noses. Your dog doesn't have any choice about the scents you choose for his environment, but you do; for him, constant "hits" of strong, artificial smells could be nearly as bad as living with someone with a 30-a-day habit would be for a nonsmoker.

GLOSSARY

Agility
In canine terms, a popular dog sport which requires the dog to move through a course with all kinds of different obstacles to go through, around, or over

Anal glands
Two pea-sized glands located inside a dog's anus, which contain a liquid which is a dog's unique scent "fingerprint," specific to him

Behaviorism
Also known as behavioral psychology, this is the study of the behavior of animals, explained in terms of conditioning rather than of the action of thoughts or emotions on behavior.

Brachycephalic
Literally "short-nosed"; the name for flatter-faced breeds of dog, such as French bulldogs and pugs

Cognition
The act of thinking and of applying intelligent thought

Cognition studies
The study of different types of intelligence in application

Commissure
The anatomical term for the corners of a dog's mouth

Cones
The receptor cells in a dog's eye that detect colors

Crepuscular
Describes animals that are especially active at dawn and dusk—the beginning and end of the day

Dichromatic
The type of vision dogs have, in which some colors are indistinguishable from one another, due to there being only two types of cone cells in the eye

Desensitization
A technique whereby a phobia is reduced by gradually creating a positive mental association with the object of fear

Domestication
The process by which most members of a previously wild species come to live alongside humans

Ethologist
A scientist trained in the study of animal behavior, preferably under natural conditions

Furaneol
A sweet-tasting compound found in a number of natural foods, such as fruit

Genome
The complete set of genes that is present in an organism

"Hard eye"
The term for the hard, fixed stare that a stressed, fearful, or aggressive dog may use to look at the object causing his disquiet

MRI scanner
Magnetic Resource Imaging scanner—a type of scanner that uses a strong magnetic field and radio waves to create detailed images of organs inside the body

Morphic resonance
A much-debated theory developed by the biologist Rupert Sheldrake, which proposes that the natural world holds inherent memories that can be passed down through living things

Olfactory epithelium
An area at the back of a dog's nose that acts as a receptacle for air breathed in and the scent molecules it contains

Oxytocin
A hormone released in mammals that enhances feelings of pleasure and well-being

Pheromone
A natural chemical produced by an animal that causes a behavioral reaction in other animals of the same species

Pinna
The exterior flap of a dog's ear

Play bow
The posture that a dog adopts when he wants to play with another dog—front paws flat on the ground, bottom in the air

Rods
The receptor cells in a dog's eye that are used to see movement and are sensitive to changes in light level

Sclera
The area of white in an eye, around the iris; not usually visible in dogs, unless they are stressed or fearful

Selective breeding
Controlled breeding, whereby specific individuals are bred together to try to ensure particular features appear in their offspring

Self-awareness
The conscious knowledge that one is an individual, different from others, with one's own thoughts and feelings

Shake-off
A brief all-over shake of the body, generally used by dogs to signify that they're concluding one activity and about to start on another—for example, a dog getting up from resting might shake off before starting to play with another

Sighthound
A type of dog that has been developed, through selective breeding, to hunt by sight

Tapetum lucidum
A reflective layer of cells behind the retina of a dog's eye, which cause a dog's eyes to sometimes reflect green in the dark

Tongue flick
A swift flick of the tongue from the side of the mouth, generally used by dogs to signal slight stress or discomfort ,

Tracking
Following a scent trail that was laid some time ago, from residual smells on the ground

Trailing
Following a fresh scent trail, by sniffing for molecules in the air

Trichromatic
The type of vision humans have, in which a full spectrum of colors can be seen, due to there being three types of cone cells in the eye

Turbinates
The bony, maze-like structure in a dog's nose which houses the scent receptors

Vibrissae
The scientifically correct name for whiskers—thick, sensitive hairs set above a dog's eyes, around his muzzle, and under his chin

Visual streak
A strip of receptor cells, packed together, that goes across a dog's retina, giving good peripheral vision

Vomeronasal organ
Also called Jacobson's organ; an area just inside the dog's nose that is used to identify pheromones

Zoopharmacognosy
A phenomenon in which animals self-medicate by selecting plants or other substances found in nature to "cure" themselves of illness or discomfort.

FURTHER RESOURCES

Bradshaw, John. *In Defence of Dogs*. London: Allen Lane, 2011.

Clothier, Suzanne. *Bones Would Rain From the Sky: Deepening Our Relationship with Dogs*. New York: Warner Books, 2005.

Coppinger, Raymond and Mark Feinstein. *How Dogs Work*. Chicago: University of Chicago Press, 2015.

Coren, Stanley. *How to Speak Dog*. New York: Simon & Schuster, 2000.

Hare, Brian and Vanessa Woods. *The Genius of Dogs*. New York: Dutton, 2013.

Horowitz, Alexandra. *Being a Dog*. New York: Scribner, 2016.

Horowitz, Alexandra. *Inside of a Dog*. New York: Scribner, 2009.

Käufer, Mechtild. *Canine Play Behavior*. WA: Dogwise Publishing, 2013.

McConnell, Patricia. *For the Love of a Dog: Understanding Emotion in You & Your Best Friend*. New York: Ballantine Books, 2007.

McConnell, Patricia. *Tales of Two Species*. WA: Dogwise Publishing, 2009.

McConnell, Patricia. *The Other End of the Leash*. New York: Ballantine Books, 2002.

Miklósi, Ádám. *Dog Behaviour, Evolution and Cognition*. Oxford: Oxford University Press, second edition, 2015.

Canine Cognition Labs that invite "citizen dog" involvement
Some university canine cognition programs invite local pets to participate in their studies. Here are a handful of options—if you're lucky enough to live near to one, take a look at their website or Facebook group to see what's involved (even if you're not nearby, the sites make interesting reading). Most studies that invite canine volunteers require proof of up-to-date vaccinations and some ask for a clean bill of health from your vet.

IN THE US:
Arizona State University, Canine Science Collaboratory
Phoenix, Arizona
caninesciencecollaboratory.blogspot.com

Duke Canine Cognition Center
Durham, North Carolina
evolutionaryanthropology.duke.edu

Eckerd College, Florida, Dog Cognition Lab
St. Petersburg, Florida
eckerd.edu

Emory University, Canine Cognitive Neuroscience Laboratory
Atlanta, Georgia
caninecognitiveneuro.wixsite.com/ccnl

Horowitz Dog Cognition Lab, Barnard College
New York, New York
dogcognition.com

University of Kentucky, Science Dogs program
Lexington, Kentucky
uky.edu/~zentall/sciencedogs.html

Yale University Canine Cognition Center
New Haven, Connecticut
doglab.yale.edu

IN THE UK
Dog Cognition Centre, University of Portsmouth
port.ac.uk/department-of-psychology/facilities/dog-cognition-centre

If you don't live near a group, look online to find any options that might be available locally.

One popular fee-charging option that anyone can join is the online test-and-questionnaire program devised by Dognition.com. It's devised by a panel of canine cognition experts headed by Brian Hare of Duke University. You test your pet's responses, then send in your results to receive a profile of your dog's cognitive strengths and personality.

INDEX

A
agility games *170–5*

air freshener *46, 183*

anal glands *37, 49*

apples *86*

aromatherapy *182–3*

autism *102*

B
BARF diets *91*

barking *72–5*

Basenji, the *74*

basset hounds *51, 52*

beagles *51, 52*

beards *36*

bedbugs *98*

behaviorism *108, 116*

Belgian Malinois *53*

Belyaev, Dmitry *16*

Bennis, Warren *103*

binocular vision *29*

"biological ladder" *18*

bloodhounds *51, 52, 54*

body language *128–41*

body temperature *21*

border collies *24*

brachycephalic dogs

   sense of smell *51*

   vision *30*

bubbles *177*

butt sniffing *48–9*

C
cancer, detection of *42, 98*

Canine Cognition Center, Yale University *120*

carrots *86*

Charleson, Susannah *41*

chimpanzees *118*

chocolate *85*

cilia *44*

cochlea *62*

cognitive studies *109, 114–15, 116*

   cognition labs *120–1*

color vision *26, 31–2*

commands *68–9*

commissure *132*

cones *26*

conservation work *103*

coonhounds *53*

Coren, Stanley *41, 47*

cross-species friendships *83*

cryptochrome *112*

D
DAID (Do As I Do) system *116, 123*

Darwin, Charles *106, 107*

Descartes, René *122*

diabetes, detecting problems *102*

digestion *21, 90*

dog–wolf experiment *17*

Dog Cognition Center, University of Portsmouth, UK *121*

Dognition Assessment, The *121*

dolphins *107, 117–8*

domestication *14–17*

drinking *89*

E
ears

   body language *134–5*

physiology *61–2*

emotions

   in dogs *122–3*

   recognition of human *34, 66–7*

epileptic fits, predicting *102*

Estep, Dan *95*

excitable dogs *167*

CREDITS

7: © Dezi

9: © Natalia Fadosova

10–11: © Kalamurzing

12–13: © Grisha Bruev

14 Left: © Iakov Filimonov

14 Right: © Eric Isselee

15: © Jeffrey B. Banke

16: © Toloubaev Stanislav

17: © Dezi

19: © Anna Issakova

20 Left: © Willee Cole Photography

20 Right: © Eric Isselee

22: © Nataliya Sdobnikova

24–5: © lidian Neeleman

27: © One Small Square

29: © MJTH

30: © Jaromir Chalabala

31: © Ireneusz Soloniewicz

33: © Budimir Jevtic

34: © Kulikova Alfiia

37: © Aspen Rock

38–29: © Liliya Kulianionak

40 Top: © Cryber

40 Bottom: © Frances A. Miller

42: © Willee Cole Photography

45: © Kellymmiller73

46: © Barna Tanko

47: © Jessica Cobb

48: © Arman Zhenikeyev

50: © Svetography

52 Top left: © NSC Photography

52 Top right: © Grigorita Ko

52 Bottom left: © Lenkadan

52 Bottom right: © Anna Titova

53 Top left: © Anetapics

53 Top right: © Best Dog Photo

53 Mid left: © Russ Beinder

53 Mid right: © Positive Me

53 Bottom left: © S.M

53 Bottom right: © FCG

55: © Sbolotova

56: © Deep Space

57: © Aerogondo2

58: © Bartosz Luka

60: © Robynrg

63: © Peter Verreussel

65 Top left: © Melory

65 Top right: © Elise V

65 Mid left: © Szasz-Fabian Jozsef

65 Center: © Pakhnyushchy

65 Mid right: © Praisaeng

65 Bottom left: © Kirsanov Valeriy Vladimirovich

65 Bottom right: © Christopher Meder

66: © Igor Normann

68: © Supercat

70: © Jeff Gammons Storm Visuals

71: © Supercat

72: © Pirita

73: © Mikkel Bigandt

74: © Nicole Hollenstein

76: © Sainthorant Daniel

77: © Anna Hoychuk

79: © Eric Isselee

80: © Jeannette Katzir Photo

81: © Supaleka P

82: © Rock and Wasp

83: © Grigorita Ko

84: © Jarva Jar

86–87: © Irina K

88: © Kastianz

89: © Wavebreak Media

90: © Kseniia Mitus

91: © Svitlana Boyko

92: © Oyls

93: © Iremt

94 Left: © Martin Rettenberger

94 Right: © Sonpichit Salangsing

96: © Jeroen van den Broek

97: © Deep Space

98: © D. Kucharski & K. Kucharska

99: © Monika Wisniewska

101: © Mona Makela

102: © Rich Carey

104: © Ekaterina Brusnika

106: © Bruce Weber

109: © Melounix

110: © ChandraSekhar

113: © Macgyverhh

115: © Couperfield

117: © Goodluz

118: © Chase Dekker

119: © Tomasz Wrzesien

120: © SpeedKingz

123: © Pavel Hlystov

125: © Maxfromhell

126: © Maratr

127: © Cynoclub

128–9: © Eric Isselee

130: © Yuri Kravchenko

131: © Petr Jilek

132 Left: © Anna Andersson Fotografi

132 Right: © Susan Schmitz

133: © Csanad Kiss

134 Left: © Vivienstock

134 Right: © Susan Schmitz

136: © Bill Anastasiou

137: © Dan Kosmayer

138: © Grigorita Ko

140 Top: © Tanatat

140 Bottom: © Wasitt Hemwarapornchai

141 Top: © Jane Salathong

141 Middle: © Eric Isselee

141 Bottom: © Kubais

142: © Lars Tuchel

143: © Olga Lis

145: © eva_blanco

166: © Alex Mladek

167: © Robynrg

168: © Elbud

169: © Vitaly Titov

170: © Dennis W Donohue

177: © Soloviova Liudmyla

178: © Jeff Thrower

179: © Oleksandr Shevchenko

180: © Ivonne Wierink

183: © Happy Monkey